Peacock Books
Editor: Kaye [illegible]

A WORKING [illegible]

At sixteen nearly every one of us has to take the decision that will decide the kind of life we are going to have. We have to choose what sort of job we are going to do.

Often the chief thing that influences us is the amount of money we will get at the end of the week, and we don't think too much about what we will be doing to earn that money, or whether it is the sort of job we could do happily and creatively for the next 40 years.

Polly Toynbee is someone who has thought about this seriously and after she had done so she set out to learn about people at work in Britain today. She discovered the sort of conditions they work under, the things that governed their choice of job, the kind of lives they lived outside their work, their ambitions, their hopes, their fears, and what they wanted from the future.

She spent months actually living this book; she worked on the shop floor of a car components factory; she joined the army; put the cream in mass-produced cakes; worked in a hospital . . . and lived with soap. '*There was soap everywhere, within a mile's radius there was enough soap in the air to make your nose twitch all the time. Sometimes it smelt like "Lifebuoy", sometimes like "Surf", and sometimes the smell was sulphurous and chemical . . . One wouldn't have been surprised if the air itself had burst into bubbles when it rained.*'

*A Working Life* is compelling reading. And anyone who is on the brink of launching themselves into an uncharted future should read it with particular interest. It does not claim to be a survey but it does make you stop and look at a way of life we seem to accept without question.

Polly Toynbee

# A Working Life

Penguin Books

Penguin Books Ltd, Harmondsworth,
Middlesex, England
Penguin Books Incs., 7110 Ambassador Road,
Baltimore, Maryland 21207, U.S.A.
Penguin Books Australia Ltd, Ringwood,
Victoria, Australia

First published by Hodder & Stoughton 1971
Published in Peacock Books 1973


Made and printed in Great Britain by
C. Nicholls & Company Ltd
Set in Linotype Pilgrim

For Peter

# Contents

# The Facts

Total population of Great Britain: 54,032,400 (June 1971 census)

Total working population of Great Britain: 24,886,000*

| | |
|---|---|
| males: | 15,885,000 |
| females: | 9,001,000 |

The *working population*, for the census, is defined as those either employed or registered as temporarily unemployed.

Numbers of Employees in Employment at June 1971 for Great Britain (index of Production Industries):

| | | |
|---|---|---|
| | | males: 7,708,000 |
| total: | 10,450,000* | |
| | | females: 2,742,000 |

Total registered unemployed April 1972: 957,600 (this represents 4·2% of all employees). 16,500 of these were 1971 school leavers who were still unemployed.

The standard weekly rate of unemployment benefit is: £6 increasing to £6.75 weekly commencing 2 October 1972.

Total retired persons receiving retirement pensions: 7,650,000* at December 1971.

The standard rate of retirement pension is £6 per week, or £9.70 for a married couple, increasing to £6.75 per week, or £10.90 for a married couple commencing 2 October 1972.

In addition to unemployment and old age payments, supplementary benefits can be claimed according to previous income, need, etc.

There is no official national minimum wage in Great Britain, but Barbara Castle, in her paper, *National Minimum Wage, An*

*Enquiry 1969* talked in terms of a minimum guaranteed wage of 32½p per hour for a 40 hour week worked. This would result in a minimum weekly wage of £13.00 for a 40 hour week worked.

The average weekly earnings for male industrial workers is £30.93.*

The average number of hours per week worked is 44.7.*

The average weekly earnings for female industrial workers is £15.80.*

The average number of hours per week worked is 37.7.*

*These figures are derived from the latest reports available from the Department of Employment and the Department of Health and Social Security and the Office of Population Censuses and Surveys, and are correct as of October 1971. At the time of going to press there were no figures available for 1972.

Chapter One

# Youth

The school leavers at the grammar school were privileged boys. They were the cream who were scooped off at eleven, turning the milk to thin useless stuff. They were the bright boys, the exceptions, the successes. But now at sixteen they wanted to leave. It had all been a mistake and it wasn't for them after all.

It was the Spring term, and they were all due to leave at the end of the Summer, after O levels. This was their first interview with the Youth Employment officer, their first brush with the world of work that they were all so eager to enter. Or at least, they were eager to get out of school. Few had special enthusiasm for work.

The school was in a Lancashire town, and was new, shining, modern and already overcrowded. The Youth Employment Officer was conducting his interviews in a stuffy store cupboard off a corner of the dining room, so that one felt his work had been relegated to somewhere low on the list of priorities. There was only just room for two chairs, and I was perched on the edge of a shelf.

It was a big school, with 600 pupils, and it was due to go comprehensive this year. In the morning the Employment Officer had arranged a careers lecture for the children. A lady journalist from the local paper talked about her work, a meteorologist talked about his, and an advertising man made a series of good jokes about his.

With a stack of files and a list of names, the officer began the interviews.

'Jones!' he called out through the half open door. A shambly, awkward boy came in at once. He had neat dark hair, chewed fingernails and patches on the elbows of his blazer. The officer was watching his every move, discreetly. 'Sit down, Jones,' he said, looking him full in the face for the first time, and then smiling. The boy sat awkwardly. There was no room for his long legs. The officer thumbed through the file on his desk.

'Well,' he said, 'I see you've put farming down on your form?'

'Yes, Sir,' said the boy, who looked a good deal younger than his age.

'Why?' asked the officer, with another smile.

'I want to work out of doors, farming or forestry. I like animals too.'

'Ever done any farming?'

'Yes, on holiday with my family. I helped on a farm in Torquay and in the Lake district.'

'What does your father do, Jones?' he asked. There was a card on the desk already filled out by the boy with all his particulars on it.

'He's an electrician.'

'Tell me, what contact have you had with animals?'

'I've got a dog, a cat and a budgie,' the boy said uneasily.

'Do you consider yourself a practical type with your hands? You've got to be if you're going to be a farmer.'

'I don't know. Probably not above average.'

'What jobs do you do round the house?' The boy looked a little taken aback at the question. He spoke his answers as if he was inventing it as he went along.

'I fixed some shelves and helped wall-papering. And I made a fence at the back with a gate.'

'Does the gate work?'

'Just about,' he answered with a brave grin. The officer then asked him what joints he'd used. What sort of gate was it? How many bars? What sort of catch? The boy stumbled and looked worried.

'Then how is your science?'

'Rotten.'

'Do you have a girl friend?'

'No.'

'Don't you like the girls?'

'I'd have them if they'd have me.' The question seemed to

me a bit rough. The officer explained later that he often asked it as it showed how adult a boy was. This boy was obviously still very much a child, he explained, and so his chosen occupation and his preferences were not to be taken too seriously. They were childish pipe-dreams.

He then went into Jones's interests. The boy listed football, athletics and drawing cartoons. What sort of cartoons? Copies of Yogi Bear and Donald Duck. The officer took a deep breath and leant back in his chair, pressing the tips of his fingers together. 'Jones,' he said, 'It seems to me you haven't taken the chances you might have done in this field. You haven't gone off in the holidays to get farming work, or at the weekends except on a few family holidays. Let's face it, you're not particularly practical – not very good with your hands – you've just helped your father a bit round the house. You're bad at sciences and maths. Farming isn't for you. I see you in shipping – the clerical side. You'd be dealing with people all day. And you might work your way up to being a quaymaster. It'd be something to work towards. You'd start in the shipping office as a clerk.' He paused to see the effect he was having. The boy was chewing his lip and looking down at his shoes. 'You see, Jones,' he went on, 'I don't interpret your interests as specifically as you do and work in a shipping office might take them all in. Talk it over with your parents. What do you think?'

The boy looked up at him and said, 'I didn't really want to work in an office, you see. I wanted to get into the country. Still, a quaymaster, I suppose that's all right.'

'Mind you,' said the officer quickly, 'I'm not saying you will be a quaymaster. That takes a lot of working towards. Still, I do see you as a clerical type.'

The boy nodded, thanked him, and got to his feet. He went out, closing the door quietly behind him. The whole interview had taken about twenty minutes.

'Well, what did you think?' the officer asked me.

'He wanted to be a farmer. Will he be all right in a big office?' I said.

'Oh, he'll be all right. That one won't change jobs. Not much initiative. He'll stay in shipping, I'd guess.'

'But,' I pointed out, 'that's not really what he wanted.'

The Youth Employment Officer took a deep breath and looked me straight in the eye. 'When you've been at this job as long as I have, you get to know what's real and what's a dream. Believe you me, the lad will settle down.' He paused, gave a small sigh and said, 'But you're right – what can I do about it?'

The officer was a man in his early forties with small sharp eyes and a frequent smile that came and was gone at the blink of an eyelid. He was one of the most hard working and energetic men I have ever met. He was a local himself and was fiercely proud of his working class background. His view of a Youth Employment Officer's job was this: he could either try to soften the blow that hits children when they leave school and enter the real world, or he could try to toughen up the children and prepare them not to flinch. The town, he explained, was a tough place, and with unemployment still rising, these boys had to have realistic aims in life, or they might find themselves out of work altogether. He was not one of the officers who consider that their work is to provide an appropriate labour force for the needs of society. He wanted the best for his boys that he could possibly get. And these, after all, were grammar school children, who would probably succeed in getting two O levels before they left. They were going into white collar work. The secondary school boys had very different prospects. The grammar boys were the privileged ones, and as long as they stuck to clerical work, there would probably always be a job for them there. 'We have,' he explained, 'tax offices, government clerical work and other big offices here, creating a large number of white collar jobs.'

But whether he was primarily interested in helping his boys, or in helping employers to get a good work-force, the results were much the same. 'It isn't my job to restructure society,' he was quick to point out. 'It is my job to try and help the kids survive in it. If the only available jobs are dreary, stultifying and unsuited to most boys, I know a few ways of making them better. I can pick out the best of a bad lot of jobs.' He could also advise on day release courses, and evening classes that might help them get promotion. For the most part, his job was to fit the boys into the existing slots, and he knew that in the end they would rub down, accept their lot and adjust their ambitions to match their horizons.

While the officer was writing up his notes on Jones, there was a knock on the door. 'I'm Kelly, Sir,' said a tall frizzy haired boy. 'Sit down Kelly,' said the officer without raising his head. He went on writing for a few minutes, occasionally glancing at Kelly out of the corner of his eye.

'Ah, Kelly,' he said at last, putting down his pen on the desk in front of him. Kelly had a habit of scratching behind one of his ears. He looked nervous and stiff.

'What do you like doing most Kelly?' the officer began. There was a blank look of panic in Kelly's eye, and nothing came to mind.

'You must like doing something, don't you?' said the officer with a quick laugh which was intended to be friendly and put him at ease, but had the reverse effect. Kelly was blushing. 'Well?'

'I like football,' said Kelly at last.

'Do you play it, or just watch it?'

'Yes, I do.'

'You play do you?'

'Yes.'

'For the school team?'

'Yes.'

'Do you support the local team? Do you often go to matches?'

'Yes.' A long pause. 'I go to home matches when I can.'

'Do you go to away matches too?'

'They're too far.' Again the officer laughed, hoping to get Kelly to unbend.

'I see you've put down travel agent or policeman, as your chosen jobs. Tell me, what's so special about those jobs?'

'I'd like to travel.'

'Have you done much travelling?'

'No. Only a few bicycle holidays.'

'But you know Kelly, travel agents stay and work in an office. They don't travel at all. Do you mean you want to be a courier and conduct tours?'

'Yes, I'd like that.'

The interview dragged on and didn't seem to be getting anywhere. The officer discovered that Kelly's father was a painter and decorator, that Kelly played cricket as well as football for the school, kept a football scrapbook, was bad at art, woodwork, maths and science and used to collect stamps.

The officer put down his pen again, rested his elbows on the desk and peered across at the boy. He began with a joke before he got down to it, 'Let's face it, Kelly, the perfect job for you would be for you to be a professional footballer.' Kelly didn't know how to take it and looked amazed.

'You see Kelly,' the officer pursued, 'you've written down here policeman or travel agent. Those are both what I call social jobs. Now do you think you are equipped for a social job? You haven't exactly got the gift of the gab. I mean I had to drag those answers out of you almost by force. Now for the jobs you've written down here, you need it. From your school report your English is much better literally than it is verbally. Written English is stronger for you than having to speak to people all the time.'

Kelly sensed what was coming, 'I don't want to work in an office. I like being out of doors. I'd like being a courier.' He hadn't spoken so many words together during the whole interview.

'Frankly, Kelly,' said the officer, 'I can't see you as a courier. You don't present to me the image of a social type. I can't see you as the life and soul of a package tour, with the responsibility for arranging everything. And you're not so good at languages are you? Now at your age I was a really cheeky lad. I'd have answered back a bit, made a few jokes, and talked my head off at an interview like this. But like you, the one thing I didn't want to do was to go and work in an office. I began on the stamp-licking bit of office life and I hated every minute of it. But I stuck it out and now I've got a really satisfying job. Think about it.' He paused. 'Now is there anything else you wanted to do?'

'Customs, perhaps.'

'I get lots of lads coming in here and saying that. Every lad wants to do it. But it takes qualifications and a lot of training. You'll get two O levels if you're lucky. Now I'm going to suggest to you that Inland Revenue would suit you to a tee. You want a social job? Well, you'd be having contact with people all the time, but in answering letters rather than meeting them, literary rather than verbal contact, which is what you are good at. I can assure you that people write some funny, rude letters to the Inland Revenue.' He paused a moment, scribbled a note and went on.

'Kelly, you know as well as I do that basically you are a clerk. Naturally you resent it. Like any fifteen year old boy worth his salt you want a job with adventure in it. I can tell you that all your worst fears about office work are well founded, at least for the first few years. If you work hard and get promotion though, it can be very rewarding. Instead of going to work straight away, you could go to college for two years and do a Public Administration course which would get you into office life at a higher level, and I would recommend that. But when it comes down to it, if the work is dull and routine, I don't blame the system or the boss, I blame you. It's all up to you. The opportunity is there.'

Kelly was shaken by this no-holds-barred summing up of his abilities and his future. He agreed that if he got enough O levels he would go on the course. Otherwise he would go straight into the Inland Revenue. He left the room politely saying 'Thank you', and still anxiously scratching behind his ear.

'I'll tell you what will happen to Kelly,' said the officer turning to me, lighting himself a cigarette. 'He won't be a policeman. He's not got what it takes. He won't do the diploma course either. He hasn't the push to go on being educated. He's a dull boy. There's not a spark in him. Perfect for office work.' He puffed at his cigarette. 'Poor Kelly. How he'll hate the first couple of years. But he'll settle.'

The Youth Employment Officer was probably right. Kelly would have been no good as a policeman, a courier or a customs man. But there he was being bundled unwillingly into a job that he would not like but would accept and stay in for the rest of his days.

At fifteen, these boys are children. They've hardly passed the stage where like all small boys, they wanted to be engine drivers or free-fall parachutists. Suddenly in one short interview, their fantasy worlds are swept away. From being the small boy who could still be anything, do anything, 'when I grow up', he finds that he has had all the opportunity he will ever have, and somehow, somewhere along the line, it slipped through his fingers without his ever having known about it. The chances are, he never had an opportunity to do something different, but like most people, believes that he had, and that he muddled it. People don't take easily to the idea that they never had a chance, (or that they did, and were cheated), that their lives were more or less predestined from the day they were born. It is too unbearable a thought to live with. In this one interview, these children are suddenly brought up short by some dim realization that where before they had opportunity always ahead of them in the world of work, they now had opportunity always behind them in the world of school, but that somehow, they had never had it at all.

The boys arrived with some idea of what went on at employment interviews, and the next boy on the list entered with his jaw set and his mind fixed on what he wanted. He looked as if he was ready for a fight. Edwards was his name, a good-looking boy, with a pink and white complexion and long curly gold hair. He looked sharper than the others, in a black corduroy jacket and a pink shirt. He walked right in and sat down.

The officer showed me the headmaster's report on Edwards. The comment written down was 'This boy is a dabbler. Picks up interests but doesn't carry them through.' The officer stubbed out his cigarette, smiled at Edwards, and began the interview.

'What are your interests then, Edwards?'

'Well, I've got a lot. I suppose classical music is the best.'

'Oh, really? What sort of classical music do you like?'

'Indian mostly,' Edwards said. The officer pursed his lips and rearranged himself in his chair.

'Now how do you get to hear Indian music?'

'I go to the university to listen, and I've got records. I go to pop concerts too and I can play the electric guitar.'

'Are you any good?'

'No, I suppose not particularly, but I like it.'

'You've written down that you want to be a commercial artist or a journalist. Well, your English isn't too good, according to your teacher, so let's forget the journalism and look at your art. How long have you been doing it?' the officer asked, although he had the answer written down in front of him. It was a technique of his when he wanted to make a point. He would ask a question, knowing the answer, when he knew that the answer would sound bad.

'Three weeks,' Edwards said. 'I've only just taken it up again. I had to give it up in the first year to do Maths and Geography. The art master thinks I'm good and I'd get A level,' he added with some defiance. He was realizing that if he was going to be dealt some body blows to his pride, he was quite within his rights to boast a little.

'But the art master doesn't think you're a genius, does he Edwards? Because he'd have told me if you were. Now, are you good with your hands?'

'I make models.'

'What sort?'

'I made a model of our team's football ground.'

'Anything else?'

'I make balsa wood models of aeroplanes.'

'Do they work? Can you get them to fly?'

'I don't like to try in case they get broken. I just like looking at them. They're so beautiful.' The officer laughed quickly and flicked through the file again.

'I see you've underlined current affairs as one of your interests? What interests you most about current affairs?'

Edwards looked a bit lost, as well one might. He seemed to be fumbling around for a subject. 'The Common Market,' he said eventually. That dreadful phrase 'Current affairs', always does conjure up some nebulous complex issue.

'Do you know the full name for the Common Market?' I was hoping he would get it right, but I couldn't remember the exact answer myself. Edwards stumbled. 'Economic Committee?' he said knowing it was wrong.

'Why does the Common Market interest you?'

'Everything's going to cost more.'

'Where do you read about it?'

'The *Daily Express*. They think we shouldn't go in. I agree.'

'What other current affairs interest you?'

'Vietnam,' Edwards said with more certainty.

'Oh, yes?' said the officer with another of those instant smiles.

'I think the Americans should get out right away.'

'And you don't mind the Communists taking over?'

'It's better to be Communist than blown to bits, isn't it?'

Then they went through the list of all Edwards's interests. He was Victor Ludorum for three years running, played in the school football team as well, and in his second year he wrote a play that was performed in front of the whole school. His father was a foreman on the shop floor at a textile works. 'Anything else?' asked the officer.

'I think a lot,' Edwards said.

'What do you think about?'

'Life, and everything else.'

He was bad at science in school but he had written down biology as an interest. 'I cut up dead animals, with a friend at home.'

'Do you kill them too?'

'No. We find them,' he said, and laughed for the first time. The officer asked if he did much reading.

'Yes, I like horror books. I'm on the waiting list to read *Das Kapital* and *Mein Kampf*. But everyone reads those.'

'They all queue up to read those. I shouldn't think one of them get beyond the first page. It sounds good in interviews,' the officer explained later.

The officer felt he had got the general picture. 'You're going to have to work hard, Edwards,' he said. 'Your report doesn't look too hopeful about getting your O levels. If you get one or two I think I could get you into an art course somewhere. I'm going to suggest that you do an Exhibition and Window Display course. It's a good course, and there are plenty of jobs in that line. But of course you must get two O levels before they'll even consider you.'

'I wouldn't like Window Display,' Edwards said. 'I want to do a design course, or a commercial artists course.'

'I wouldn't advise it. You've got to be marvellous at it to do well in that field. I can see you're the artistic type, and I'd like to combine that side of your personality with the practicalities of life. And I don't think an art school would take you.'

In the end they agreed to wait until they saw his results before a final decision was made. He left the room with some of the defiance gone, but still looking determined.

'What will happen to him?' I asked. 'He seems brighter than the others.'

'Seems, yes,' said the officer. 'He's full of enthusiasm and he's a livelier lad than most, but when it comes down to it, where does that lead you? I mean he can talk all right, and he's good at interviews. That's half the battle. He knows what to say and presents himself well. He might be able to con his way through a bit. Most of the lads appear at their worst at an interview. This one was at his best. But I don't think he's got much push. He hasn't really done anything for himself. He hasn't set out to get himself into an art school. He doesn't really know anything about current affairs, although he'd underlined it three times. The Common Market? Vietnam? Hadn't a clue. As for "classical" music, all he meant was some flipping Indian playing a sitar. We shall see. I reckon he'll fall down on his exams, and he'll either take my advice, or drift from job to job and be unsatisfied the rest of his life.'

The Youth Employment Officer, sitting at his desk, tried to look at the boys through the eyes of the world. To take his words at face value would be quite wrong. He was not a philistine hater of youth and new ideas. He was a great football fan, and was anti the war in Vietnam. He had nothing against Indians or their music, or against people wanting to be artists. He said he had been a wild jazz enthusiast himself. But that was not the point.

'If that lad wants to be an artist, he'll go off and be one, without my say-so or anyone else's, and good luck to him too. I'd be glad. But that's not my job. He needs the other side put to him, and I don't think he's tough enough to go off and do it.'

He was not judging the boys' views, but what he thought they represented. Edwards seemed to him like a boy going through all the fashionable crazes, Kelly a child looking for adventure.

He was looking at them not as a teacher or a father, but as their employers would see them when they came to apply for work.

I attended these interviews not in order to examine the work of Employment officers but to get some insight into the way in which children enter work. The average child, by the time he is fifteen and leaving school, has little or no choice. I chose a group of children who were relatively privileged. Indeed, throughout this book I have tried not to seek out the worst off or the very poor or the worse places of employment. I tried to choose reputable firms where working conditions are less than appalling and more or less average. I have avoided the back-street sweat-shops, the bottom-stream children, the poorest old age pensioners. I have written about work as it is experienced by most people – unskilled and semi-skilled work at neither its best nor at its worst.

In fact these grammar school boys were privileged only in name and status. They were destined to become and remain white collar workers, with the added status that goes with office work. They would be paid less than a good many of the boys who leave secondary school at the same time. There was no reason to think that their jobs would be any more rewarding or fulfilling than the manual jobs of the secondary schoolboys. In fact, this particular Employment officer was more enthusiastic about the secondary boys than he was about these.

'The secondary boys at the top of their class are successes. They've done well at school,' he said. 'These ones are failures, and are regarded by their other classmates as drop-outs. The secondary boys have been more prepared for leaving school. These ones come straight out of latin and geography lessons that have done them no good at all. And because they have the "Grammar school boy" label stuck round their neck, and they were marked out at the beginning as little gentlemen they wouldn't be allowed by their families to take other sorts of jobs. They've moved up a social notch from their parents, and everyone wants to keep it that way, even if it isn't in the child's interest. Of course there are so many office jobs here that that doesn't apply so much. It's the other jobs that are in short supply. Post and tax offices will take almost anyone. All the same, I prefer dealing with the secondary school boys. They're a more lively lot.'

The Employment officer was a self-educated man from a working-class background. A strong side of his nature inclined him towards proseletizing working-class life and values. He was proud of his background and everything it represented. He wanted his boys to stay his boys. He had no admiration for the middle classes and as a result his aspiration for the boys was cramped. The working class perpetuates itself by being administered by working class people. A university man might have encouraged some of these boys in their wilder fancies, and have laid less emphasis on the hard realities of life. Perhaps in the long run that would not be in their interests. But it must, nevertheless, have an inhibiting effect on class mobility if teachers and Employment officers work on the principle that 'working class is best'. This officer said, sadly 'In twenty-five years' time, it won't be worth being a Youth Employment Officer here. They'll all be middle class. At the moment anyone who makes any money moves to the town next door, but we'll get like that in the end.'

There were a few more interviews. A tiny boy who looked only twelve had already fixed himself up with an office job, one agreed to try a printer's office, three more for tax offices, one for a Public Administration course. Then it was four o'clock. The officer packed up his files and we set off back to his office.

The Youth Employment Bureau was a curious old derelict building. It had once been a hospital. His office was a small cramped dingy place, with faded green institutional paint half way up the wall. There was a notice board in the room on which were pinned advertisements for different trades, dry cleaning, dairies, nursing, and a series of rather chilling mottoes were scattered all around. 'Many a false step is made by standing still.' 'Some people turn up their sleeves – some their noses.' 'Hard work is the yeast that raises the dough.' 'To miss a goal is not necessarily to fail; many a match is won by a try.' 'All are not hunters who blow the horn,' and other such uplifting sentiments.

Here, every evening the Youth Employment held a 'surgery'

for young workers up to the age of eighteen. Many of them he knew personally, having seen them before they left school, and having got some of them jobs. They waited in the passage outside where there was still a lingering smell of disinfectant.

A boy came into the room. He had short dark hair and was wearing a coat with the collar turned up. He had left school a year ago, wanting to be a farmer. He had been told that he needed chemistry and a few other O levels, and he had now managed to get these, at night school while working in a factory. He had just been in hospital and off work for three months with a broken back. He said 'a mate at work knocked me downstairs, by mistake. When I went back this week they gave me my cards.' The officer promised to find him a job on a farm, as he was obviously determined, and he would then get him into an agricultural college later.

'You see,' said the officer triumphantly, when he had gone, 'they don't always take my advice. I told that one to do office work, but he wasn't having it, and he's worked and shown that he really wants to be a farmer. It isn't just a dream. He's a good lad.'

The next boy in the queue was not a 'good lad'. But the officer smiled at him, and laughed quite benevolently afterwards. He was seventeen, with long hair down his back. 'I call him Jesus Christ,' joked the officer. He had been working in a supermarket as a packer. He spoke defiantly, but in a very soft and sing-songy voice, designed to madden, probably. He had been at grammar school but had consistently refused to have anything to do with a 'career'. He had worked almost all the time since then, but had drifted from one casual job to another. He was now earning £6.90 a week.

'Can't I persuade you to do something a little more worth while?' said the officer, as if he had been through it all so many times that he was not going to try particularly hard.

'I find it difficult to think career-wise,' was the answer. The boy began to roll up a cigarette. 'I just want a job with a bit more money because I want to leave home and get a flat with some friends.'

'I shouldn't think I could get you one earning more than

£7.50 a week. That to me is below subsistence level. I don't think you'd survive in a flat. You said your parents were chucking you out. Is that still so?'

'Maybe they won't let me back tonight,' he said with a shrug, licking up the cigarette paper.

'Are you still going off to Israel?' the officer asked. The boy shook his head. 'I sent you to that supermarket job because you just wanted something temporary before you went away.'

'The supermarket didn't like the way I look.'

'Well then, we'll leave it at that. What sort of job are you prepared to accept?'

'Anything, so long as there's enough money. I'll go in a factory or anywhere.'

'Look, give me some kind of a hint. I've got to nail you down to something.'

'Any job is a career.'

'Oh, all right, I'll see what I can find. When do you finish at your present job? Saturday? I'll find you something by then.' The boy smiled, nodded and sidled out, with a vague wave in the way of a good-bye. The officer leant back in his chair, laughed, and shook his head, but he looked a little cross. 'He only comes in here to show off. If he really wanted any old job, he wouldn't have to bother with coming to the Bureau. He wants to show off his independence, and make sure that we are still trying not to let him waste his abilities. Oh, I don't know. Who knows? Maybe he's happy.'

2

That Youth Employment Officer was a tough and forthright man. His interviewing techniques will perhaps seem brutal. His abrasive aggressive manner with the boys might shock some people. At first I thought him like a steam-roller, systematically flattening out every spark, every mark of individuality in the boys. Yet he cared passionately, fiercely about the well-being of his children. He believed the best way to handle them and help them was to shake them up, to make them think for themselves if they were capable of it.

There are only a certain amount of jobs, and there are roughly the same number of children leaving school. If a Youth Employment officer decided that he wanted only the very best for his children, and he managed to squeeze his whole brood into the few satisfying, interesting and worthwhile jobs that there are, he would not really be gaining anything in the long run. It would only mean that the children from the school next door would have to take up the boring useless jobs. A Youth Employment officer, unfortunately, cannot create jobs. He is only an agent. He can't provide the employers with special children, or the children with special jobs. His interviewing style is of secondary importance. His job is to place children in society as it is. He can only hope to persuade them to accept it and become reasonably happy in it.

But in the back of his mind, this officer was angry. He didn't like pushing these children into unsuitable work. He admitted to me that he was rough with them in the hope that they might put up a fight. He wanted them to shout back at him, to refuse to be fobbed off with a third best existence. He was half wanting them to be goaded into saying 'No'. Not all Employment officers are like him. Many are gentle and sympathetic and resigned. But it doesn't make much difference. The end result is more or less identical.

In another Youth Employment Bureau in a South Yorkshire city, I sat for a day with an officer so timid and gentle that his clients hardly knew they were being interviewed. The city is used to full employment, and a diversity of jobs. The Employment officers have a freer hand and an easier task. But it is still a difficult job.

Eighty-five per cent of the Youth Employment Bureaux throughout Britain are attached to local authorities and are not part of the civil service. When Bureaux were first set up local authorities could choose whether to control them themselves or whether to let the Department of Employment take them over. Only fifteen per cent handed them over to the Department, mostly in rural areas. At the age of eighteen the young worker is transferred from the bureau to the Employment Exchange. This means, claim the officers in the Employment Exchanges, that the youth bureaux do not really benefit from the wider knowledge of the employment scene available to the exchanges. It also means that there are liable to be regional variations in the efficiency of the service, depending on the attitude of the local authority. But most Youth Employment officers believe that the children are most likely to benefit from a service that is treated as part of education and not as part of industry. All agree that the main disadvantage of the present system is that on reaching their eighteenth birthday the young workers are shunted from one small office that deals specifically with their problems to a much larger, more impersonal establishment. Some say the Youth Employment Bureaux should be incorporated into the exchanges, getting the benefit of a full view of jobs and better knowledge of the prospects and future in certain industries, and others that the bureaux should keep the children until they reach the age of twenty-one.

In this particular Yorkshire city the Youth Employment officers conduct four meetings with parents and children in school from the third year until they leave. In the final year, the children get an average of one and a half interviews with the officer. After starting work, about eighteen per cent of the boys and about fifteen per cent of the girls come back to the bureau for further advice.

The Y.E.B. was in a shabby one floor building on the main road out of the city. Further down the street was the Employment Exchange, like a larger and grimmer senior school.

The officer I sat with was a tall awkward man with a thin red face, bulbous eyes and a soothing voice. Gentle and kindly, he called his clients by their Christian names, repeating the names over and over as an added gesture of goodwill, 'Well, Jean,' 'Now tell me, Jean,' 'Jean, it seems to me.' In his tiny thin-walled office he sat quietly nodding his head, listening and asking questions in an apologetic tone. His interviews were in striking contrast to the Lancashire officer's. Except that in the end, the results were much the same.

A pretty girl with long brown hair and a childish un-made-up face came in and sat down, carefully crossing her legs, sitting up straight in her chair, and purposefully resting her hands on her knee.

'Hello, Jean, I don't think we've met before. But I've got your papers here, if you'll excuse me while I just cast an eye over them?' Jean smiled. 'Ah, yes, Jean. Now you were a junior clerk with that finance company. What can I do for you?'

Jean, who was seventeen but looked three years younger, crossed and re-crossed her legs, took a small breath and said, 'Well, you see, I've always wanted to be a telephonist. When I left school there weren't any jobs and I wondered if you had any now?'

'That may not be too easy, but I'll see what we can do. Now, would you mind just telling me a little about the job you're in at the moment?'

'Well, most of the day I'm doing filing, a bit of Xeroxing, a bit of typing, and sometimes I get one hour a day on the switchboard when the other girl goes out to dinner.'

'Tell me, I know it sounds a silly question, but what's so special about switchboard operating?' he asked. Jean smiled again. She seemed to be making a tremendous effort to sound grown up and a little refined.

'I just like speaking to people on the phone. I use my brother's telephone sometimes, and I like that.' She looked down at her fingernails. 'I've always tried to speak well, you see. You have to for that job.' She did speak well too, carefully ironing out as much of her Northern accent as she could. 'I did think of elocution lessons, but I never got round to it.'

The officer laughed and complimented her on her voice. 'The trouble is Jean, the G.P.O. don't train telephonists any more, since they went on to S.T.D. and most other places want girls with experience.'

'I did ring up all the hospitals as they need people, but they wouldn't take me when they heard I was only seventeen and didn't have any experience.'

'Oh, that was a very good idea. I see you've really been trying. I do hate to disappoint you, but I think the best I can do is find you general office with relief switchwork.'

'Filing again?'

'I'm afraid Jean, that I really haven't got anything else for you, but I could put you on the list of telephonists. How would that be?'

'Well, I suppose so,' she said looking disappointed.

'But I'll tell you what, Jean, why don't we find you a job with a day release, and you could learn to be a secretary?'

'Go to college? Oh no, I wouldn't want to.'

'Of course it's entirely up to you. But if I was you, I'd always go for the jobs that have a day release, because it shows that they're good employers.'

Eventually she agreed on a job in a small civil engineers' office, but she left the room without much enthusiasm, thanking the officer who apologized and wished her the best of luck.

'I would love to have found her a telephonist's job. Such a sweet girl,' he said, turning to me. 'Of course, I would have pushed the idea of further education a bit more strongly if I hadn't had her school report. They say she's not nearly as intelligent as she seems. She probably only just about holds her own in the job she has.'

I asked how long school reports were kept. 'Three years, and then they're destroyed,' he said. 'On the whole they're pretty accurate, and we get to know the teachers.'

The school, it seemed, had not only failed to give Jean a proper start in life, but was now holding her back. After all a great many children do very badly at school, find the atmosphere quite uncongenial, but succeed as soon as they leave. In many cases the school report might bear no relation to a child's aptitudes at work but the report would provide the bulk of the material the employment officer has to go on.

Next came a boy, tall, miserable looking, with a toothbrush moustache. He sat down with an air of slightly aggressive determination and began to talk very fast and confusedly, stumbling over his words.

'I'm not getting anywhere, you see. I want to get on in life. I want a job with a future. All these jobs I've had, they won't let me get on. It's no good having jobs that get you nowhere all the time,' he said in one breath, glowering at the officer from under his moustache.

'Well, Michael, tell me what you've been doing since you left school,' said the officer softly, trying to stem the flood of anxious words. Michael was twisting his fingers together. He took a deep breath and said, 'I'm working at a big supermarket you see. They call it Provisions Assistant, but it isn't the job it sounds. I'm stacking dog biscuits and soap packets all day on to the counters. There's no promotion, no training. I tell them I want a chance to get on and they don't do anything about it. I thought Provisions Assistant would mean something to do with buying but it's just stacking.'

'What did you do before that?'

'When I left school? I went to work with my Dad. He has a small firm. I was rewinding transformers. But my brother was there, and we didn't get on. He shouted at me all the time. I left, and my father doesn't want to know any more. My brother doesn't work there now. I might have done some good if I'd stayed, but my Dad doesn't want to know.'

'Have you had any other jobs, Michael?' he asked gently.

'I worked in a bakery.'

'Why did you leave?' the officer asked.

'It was boring work, and no prospects. After that I went as a van assistant in a laundry helping deliveries, but I had an accident in it, and I broke an arm and a leg and I was off work for six months.'

'I see. Now tell me, you haven't been to a Youth Employment officer before?'

'No. When I was leaving school I was dead set on working with my Dad, so I didn't need a job. I found the other jobs myself.'

'What do your parents think you should do? Have you talked to them about it?' he asked.

'Well, I don't know. I don't think my Dad's bothered. My Mum thinks I should get a good job and get on.'

'So what sort of job would you like now, Michael?'

'Something in the grocery trade. I want to get on to the buying side.'

'I see. Now just let me look at your file a moment, just so that

I can keep it up to date with everything you've done since you left school.' He went out of the room to find it.

'You see,' Michael said when he came back, 'they say other industries are important, but when it comes to it, food is the only thing everyone has to have. That's why I'm interested in it.'

'Have you always been keen on a job before you actually do it?'

'Yes, I suppose I get disillusioned.'

'All right, fair enough. Now would you mind if we just go back to your school for a moment? What subjects did you like?'

'History. English too.'

'Why history?' the officer asked with a smile. Michael looked a bit stuck for words and he stammered. 'Um, well it's interesting. You've got to know what went on,' he paused awkwardly. 'I mean another thing, you might suddenly find the Duke of Marlborough was your ancestor or something.' The officer smiled.

'Well, Michael, I think you're right to want a change of job. That supermarket chain do tend to work young people into the ground. They're not very good employers. I think the answer for you would be to work in the Co-op. There's one just near where you live. They're nice people and I think you'd have a better time there. They'd give you a day release course too, which is always a good thing.'

'Would they let me get on?' the boy asked. The officer didn't quite answer. 'They're very good employers,' he said.

An interview with the Co-op was arranged immediately over the telephone – no shortage of vacancies, and the boy went away looking quite pleased, still dreaming of someday being a Lord Sainsbury.

Now the Co-op was exactly the sort of job I would have expected this kindly officer to have picked out. He was a gentle and considerate man who didn't like to expose his children to the harsh commercialism of an independent chain. The Co-op was an ideal solution to him.

'I feel so sorry for that poor boy,' said the officer to me. 'His father started his own small business and obviously puts a lot of pressure on his sons. Poor Michael just isn't up to it. I don't think he really has much ambition. He just needs a job that will suit him.' He glanced down at the file. 'You see, he was hopeless at school. Bottom stream.'

I asked what he'd learn on his day release from the Co-op.

'He'll do a basic grocery course.' What was that? 'He'll learn about the grocery trade on the sales side. How to handle money and give change, how bacon slicers work, that sort of thing.'

'Do you think he'll get on?' I asked.

'He'll settle and be quite happy, I hope. Otherwise he'll just keep changing jobs.' The officer leant back in his chair. 'You see you must be careful not to expect too much of these boys and girls. You must be careful not to put them into jobs that will be too hard for them. They'll be unhappy and worried.'

There was a knock on the door. 'Come in,' called the officer, straightening up the papers on his desk. A tall boy came in, curly brown hair, inky fingers, shabby blazer and a tattered school satchel under one arm. 'This one's a bad boy I'm afraid,' he said with a laugh. The boy laughed too and put down his satchel. 'Sit down, Richard,' he said. 'This boy's at the grammar school,' he said turning half towards me. The boy grinned again. 'He got seven O levels last Summer and now he wants to leave.' He paused and looked at the boy again. 'I suppose,' he said, 'that everyone has already told you that you're making a mistake?' Again the boy smiled and said that he wasn't going to change his mind.

'I want a commercial apprenticeship, you see. I want to be a trainer manager.'

'Tell me, Richard, what does your father do?'

'He's a train driver.'

'I hope you'll excuse me asking, but there's enough money at home is there? That's not why you're leaving?'

'Oh no. They say I should stay but I can leave if I want. But I don't like school. I don't like the discipline. A sixth form college wouldn't be better either. I just don't want to go on learning.' The officer pointed out that the school had tipped him for a university place. He shrugged and said, 'I don't fancy it.'

'Oh well, we'd better get down to it then. Still with those O levels you can afford to pick and choose a bit with the apprenticeships.'

But the boy was so eager that he was delighted with the sound of the first one that the officer suggested. It was a small and dingy engineering office. The officer probably chose a particularly unattractive one in the hope that when the boy saw it, he would change his mind. The apprenticeship would mean learning about the whole office side of the business and doing a two year diploma day release course. The boy didn't seem to listen much to the details. Work in itself seemed glamorous to him. He had only a hazy idea of what 'going into industry' meant and he had a very clear idea that leaving school meant being grown up. Schools' lack of fore-sight in failing to make life more adult and enjoyable for their sixth formers must create a great many unnecessary drop-outs.

'You know, Richard, if you find work bores you, there's nothing whatever to stop you going back to your A levels.'

The boy got up and left with a confident smile, an interview with the firm already arranged. As he was going out of the room I wanted to call him back and take him with me to see the factories and offices I had seen and worked in. I should like to have shown him the cake bakery, the scourers department of Lever Brothers, the shop floor at Lucas's. Wouldn't he then change his mind?

Chapter Two

# Cakes

Outside it is a mellow September morning. The misty sun glances off the corrugated iron, the rusty fire-escapes, the rows of vans, the stacks of oil drums and the tarmac. Fork-lift trucks are at work already, shifting the piled-up cake containers. Service engineers lean against the doorways, smoking and laughing and whistling at the girls in white.

It is seven forty a.m. The Cake Bakery girls hurry across the large factory compound. It is five minutes to clocking-in time. The girls don't look round at the men, but hurry down to the basement of their building, taking a last breath of fresh air, a last drag on the morning's first cigarette.

There is a bustling and pushing at the clock. Then the machines start up, at exactly quarter to eight. The girls start the actions they will repeat thousands of times that day.

The noise is fearful, threatening and relentless. Like a horrible symphony orchestra, the sounds mix together in perfect rhythms, each bar repeated exactly over and over again. One sound is like the air brakes of a lorry on a hill. Another is an old engine letting off steam at the end of a long journey. Four packing machines are crashing huge hammers down on to metal plates very fast. The belts chug loudly and evenly, as the two slicers hiss. Overhead a line of clattering hangers circles the room, taking the finished cakes to the floor above. Somewhere in the background a loudspeaker is playing music, but only occasional strains of it can be heard. When the machines stop, the music sounds loud, showing how noisy the machinery is. There is no conversation, only occasional shouted commands, often repeated several times before they can be understood.

From seven forty-five until four-fifteen, apart from half an hour for lunch and two quarter-hour tea breaks, the girls worked down there for five days a week, doing one small action to every cake that came down the line – over and over, for a basic wage of what was then £10.65. It has since gone up to £14.25, a remarkable rise of nearly 33 per cent.

In fact the jobs do get changed around from time to time. I started off on one of the nicer ones. I sat at the conveyor belt slipping a piece of cardboard under each cake as it came down the line. At first it was difficult to keep up. An uneconomic movement, a fumble, and four cakes were gone without cards. I got up to chase the four cakes, eight more appeared, and for five minutes or so I had to work at twice the speed to work my way back to where I was sitting before. But it only takes half a day or so to learn how it's done, and soon it became quite automatic. The frenzy had quite worn off by the end of the first day, and then there was only the monotony and the aching arms.

Later I moved to another job on the line, as the girl who usually did it had left. I wasn't surprised. It was the nastiest job in that department. As the cake came out of a machine that had sliced it into three layers, two streams of artificial cream were poured over the layers. I had to stack the layers up again – a messy and very tiring job. The cakes are heavy and the cream is slippery.

Anyone who has worked at all in a factory knows how deathly conveyor belt work is. At first it is difficult to keep up, and when you're tired it is quite merciless. After a while, when you have become fairly used to it, the fact that you can't work faster is also infuriating. Sometimes, when things are going well, you feel that you could go fast for a while, and maybe slow up later when you were tired. But no, you must work at exactly the prescribed speed, making exactly the same movements, being careful to be as economical with energy as possible, learning not to put your back into it but to use only your arms, learning how to use the wrists the same way every day so the muscles are strengthened and don't go on aching. It looks so easy, and it is, but it's important to make it as easy as possible. One false move repeated three thousand times is a painful mistake.

I had often wondered what people thought about, working on assembly lines all day. The answer is nothing. The work needs just enough concentration to keep the mind occupied. I had thought it would be a time when I could sit and think for hours on end. But my mind was blank. The monotony permeates every corner of the brain. The rhythm deadens every thought. I found myself repeating tables endlessly just for the sake of doing something. One afternoon I got up to 500 times 500. From the miserable and expressionless faces of the other girls, I doubt whether they were thinking much either. Just cakes and more cakes and more cakes.

Sometimes the machines would break down. If the right machine broke down in the right place, it meant you had a rest. If the wrong one broke down, it meant you worked twice as fast. The other break in routine came when the cakes changed colour. Every day we had to get through a specified number of cakes of different colours. To start with, they were striped pink, yellow and white. Then there was chocolate, then a plain one with cream and jam. This was the worst for me, as the jam didn't stick two layers together as firmly as the cream. It meant using both hands at once to get the cake straight instead of using each hand in turn, which was much less tiring.

Everyone longed for the right machine to break down. Everyone was watching the clock for tea and lunch breaks. But the breaks weren't set for any particular time. We were given our breaks when the cake ran out, or when we had to wait for the next lot of cream, or at the end of one colour of cake. This meant that sometimes we were given a tea break three quarters of an hour after starting in the morning, which meant working through non-stop from quarter to nine until lunch, which might not be until one o'clock. Then the tea break might be at two o'clock, almost straight after lunch.

There was no trade union in this factory, except for a few skilled engineers. None of the women belonged to a union. Had there been one, I am sure the question of tea breaks at the right times is the sort of thing that would very quickly have been put right. There have been strikes about just that question. I wonder if the people who complain about the frivolity of tea-break disputes have any realization of what it is like to work at repetitive tiring jobs?

Quarrels flare up quickly, for no apparent reason. A tiny old man sat like a small bundle on a high stool, feeding the ready creamed cakes into a machine that cut them into four. He suddenly started to yell and scream, louder than the machines, at a tall African girl who was putting the cakes from a trolley on to the belt for him. She screamed back at him. Neither could hear what the other was saying. Eventually the supervisor came and bawled out both of them. Later, at lunch, the girl told me that he'd been complaining to her that she was putting the cakes out too fast or too slow, and that she never did it right. 'He's always on at me,' she said. 'Nothing I bloody do is right.'

When she said, 'He's always on at me,' she didn't mean that he actually said anything, because he wouldn't have been heard. All communication is non-verbal, but it's communication all the same. She meant that he'd been angry with her, that he'd been glowering at her, grabbing the cakes away from her before she had let go, taking the cakes especially fast to show that she was going slower than he wanted her to go. She had got angry and gone slower still, not seeing any reason for speeding up, had held on to each cake a fraction of a second too long, had given a slightly diffident look around the room while languidly handing out the next one, pretending not to notice that he wanted to go faster. And all this was practically unnoticeable to anyone not working on that particular line at that particular time. It is such a fractionally small delay, or speeding up, that an observer couldn't see it or time it.

I found myself being maddened with rage by the woman sitting opposite me. She was a large, rather sour middle-aged West Indian. She had been there for years, and was controlling the flow of the cream machine. It was also her job to put the top layer of the cake on to the second layer, as it came out of the machine. I had to lift both layers and put them on to the third. As we sat opposite one another, the speed at which she worked determined the rate at which I had to work. As she did her bit first, it meant that I had to do mine later, and a little further down. If she was slow, or held on to the cake for an extra moment, I had to lean further down the line, which was uncomfortable and she knew it. We never spoke a word, but there was a great deal of aggression between us. She would hold on to the cakes longer and longer, and sometimes I would even have to get up and walk down the line to catch up. We also had to clean up the spare cream that often came out on to the belt. She was quicker than me with the palette knife and would clean up my bit, too. Then I would get better at it and poach on to her bit. The point of this was that sometimes no cream came out of the machine, and we had to spread it ourselves from the cream in the bowl beside us. The cream in the bowl was the spare cream we had gleaned off the belt, so we had to collect as much of it as we could.

All this sounds insane. Of course it is, and it is what preoccupies everyone in assembly line work. Ask what we were thinking – we were thinking about how infuriating the person we worked with was, or we were waiting for the next bit of spare cream to spill on to the conveyor belt. Mad, obsessive, and utterly pointless. If the work is of minimal interest, so the thoughts and preoccupations of the mind will match it exactly. A stupid boring job makes a stupid boring mind.

At this particular factory, the turnover of labour was rapid. Very few girls had been there long. Most of them were married with children. Rosanne, the tough supervisor, had been there for over eighteen years. The work seemed to obsess her completely. One couldn't imagine what she did away from the factory. She never talked about anything else. She was a big Irish woman who talked without stopping, swore a good deal, grumbled and yelled but was definitely on the side of the girls rather than the management. She had a habit of touching everyone at every opportunity, putting her big arms around them, straightening their hair-nets, carefully wrapping aprons round them, clutching their waists affectionately. But not many of the girls liked her. She didn't like the men under her care, and they kept as clear of her as they could.

The men seemed to work a great deal less hard than the women. About ten of them were wandering around the assembly line, moving trolleys, filling up the cream machine, mending the machines if they broke down. They had none of the pressure of forced assembly work. At this time they earned a basic wage of £13.75 a week, more than the women. This has since gone up to £16.50 for a 40-hour week, another large rise in a short time. The women's wages have risen by 13 per cent more than the men's, a step nearer to equal pay. This is an uncharacteristic move in wage scales for industry as a whole.

A tall and exquisite Indian woman wandered up and down the line. She was heavily scented – a marvellous strong Eastern scent – and as she passed, even the smell of the cakes and cream was eclipsed. She had a long neck, silk trousers and a caste mark on her forehead. She was a quality inspector.

Sometimes if we finished our consignment of cakes early in the day, we would be moved up to another department, away from the basement, to work which was much less tiring. On the top floor another kind of chocolate cake was made. It was quiet there, and the windows looked out on to roofs across the whole factory. There was time and quiet to talk.

One day I worked with Barbara, an ageing Scottish woman from Aberdeen. She talked all the time, mostly too softly to be heard. I thought at first that it was directed at me, but I don't think she expected answers. All day long she talked to herself. I only caught part of it, and felt I was intruding. The others laughed at her and said she was soft in the head. She had a daughter of thirteen and lived with her in a small room, costing three pounds a week. She hadn't enough money for a bus fare to work and would set out at six thirty in the morning to walk the whole way. She said most of her money went on drink. Five pints a night and a cherry brandy to finish up with. 'My God, you need something, though, don't you?' she said to me, looking me hard in the eye. How did she manage? 'I have friends I see sometimes,' she said. She talked for the most part about drink, comparing gin to whisky, asking if I'd ever had an egg flip with rum, or a creme de menthe and gin. The rest of what she said was mumbled. She worked very fast and had been there a year. She hated it. 'I'd spit in the cakes, I would,' she said one afternoon. 'They pay you bugger all and they use up your life. And they have spies.' She looked around with suspicion. 'You watch it, dear, spies everywhere.' She wouldn't explain. In a strange way, she was much the most articulate of the women that I met there.

None of the others liked it, but she was passionate in her hatred. 'It's criminal. It's no better than prison,' she said. 'I'd like to blow the place up. But they have spies.'

A very high proportion of the girls were coloured. One social worker said it was because coloured families pay such high rents and mortgages that more of the women have to work. It seemed bad enough to me to have to get up at six thirty to get to work. Most of them were up at six to cook breakfast and leave it in the oven for their children. Some of them had young children that they left with minders during the day. When they came back in the evening there was all the housework to be done, the greasy breakfast plates still on the table, and the evening meal to be cooked. I don't know how they had the strength. I was exhausted by the time I got home. Most of them said they went to bed at nine or earlier. Work was almost the whole of their lives.

I was horrified by the work, and became depressed within a few days – tired, and bored. In the evenings I had meant to take notes, but was too deadened by the day to do anything except watch television. That kind of work gets right into the system. You can't shake it off when you get home and settle down to something rewarding or creative. Sociologists who examine the so-called leisure problem might find the answer lies in work. What will people do with more leisure time? Look how they waste it now in bingo halls, the palais, the pub and down the bowling alley. Why don't they go home and read a good book? Throw a pot or two in the pottery at the local arts centre? Join the local operatic club? Have play readings and chess tournaments? Take evening classes, learn a language or two. Paint pictures of sunsets in the municipal park? Read poetry beside the fire, or even write it? Couldn't they do something worthwhile to enlighten their existence? Couldn't they expand their minds in the evenings, so that they wouldn't mind about the drudgery of their work? Can't they spend their money on anything other than drink and the dogs?

Such William Morris thoughts about the worker who loves to weave and paint of an evening are a long way from how things really happen. Of course there are a few splendid and amazing workers who do manage to do interesting things on the side, but the sort of strength of character, the determination and the sense of identity needed are immense. It seems to me, from my own experience, that the level of interest in one's work corresponds exactly with the level of interest in one's leisure. If I am working hard in *The Observer* office, and am interested in what I am doing, I feel twice the incentive in the evening to work at my own writing. If I have been bored all day with nothing to do, as is often the case in journalism, then I will be bored in the evening too. When I was working in the cake factory, I was bored to the point of desperation. In the evening there was nothing I wanted to do except watch television for hours on end. I didn't want to paint, or write, or have interesting conversations. My mind had gone blank, had adapted itself to the level of activity required of it during the day. The mind is like a stomach: it expands or contracts to suit the requirements. If it isn't required to stretch itself, it will tailor itself neatly to become a machine. Mine did it frighteningly fast, and I, after all, have the advantage of education and other intellectual stimulants.

Almost more depressing than anything were the few very young girls who worked there. There were two particularly touching ones down in the basement. They looked twelve, and could have passed for nine. They were tiny, baby-faced and frightened-looking. They kept to themselves and never spoke to the older women. At fifteen they had come straight from school to this factory. There were almost no prospects of promotion or of getting training for anything better. Perhaps they would leave and move on to a better job, but I felt they would probably stay. The firm puts out a lot of leaflets for young school-leavers, written in a sickeningly patronizing and chummy style. One of them has a picture of an attractively smooth young boy and girl on the cover and is headed, 'Would you like work-mates like these?' It goes on, 'You want to work with people. And if you like them, really date them. Make great friends. Have some money to spend, to dress in gear clothes, to get out to the swinging places. When you leave school you suddenly grow up and you want to make the most of it.' Another one, called 'We've got a bright future mapped out for you,' says, 'Come in and see for yourself. We've opened a brand new employment centre where we invite you to come in for a chat and a cuppa. It's just as simple as that! Bring along Mum and Dad if you like!' The attraction of factory jobs of this kind to the very young school-leaver is obvious. At the age of fifteen she can step straight out of her school tunic and 25p a week pocket money, to earning more or less the same as her mother. Naturally, Youth Employment Officers try as hard as they can to persuade school-leavers to take apprenticeships; but apprentices of 16 only earn a fraction of what a factory would pay.

The recruiting office was a pretty bleak place. The posters and leaflets brightened a featureless room. Two austere people, looking like school teachers, sit perched on stools behind a counter, perusing the queue of would-be employees with great distaste. They don't assume that everything they are told is true. They repeat the same question several times, to check. The woman in glasses turned down the boy ahead of me in the queue with brisk satisfaction because he admitted to having two jobs in the last two months. Why shouldn't he move around? It must help to make life a little more bearable when work is as boring as that.

Then there was the hygiene inspection. We undressed and were given paper hospital gowns. I went into the surgery. A tired nursing sister was there. She asked me questions, not listening to the answers, crossing off the Noes before I had replied. Dermatitis? Hepatitis? Haemorrhoids? Registered disabled? She took my blood pressure. She tested my eyes, but did nothing about the fact that, short-sightedly, I couldn't read much below the first line on the card. Then that was all.

Coming out of the medical I found an old woman on the stairs picking up a dog end and stuffing it into her pocket as she puffed and wheezed her way up. She might have made use of the rule that allowed us to eat as much cake as we wanted on the premises. Why don't they eat the cake? Only the hungry could have looked at the stuff after making it all day and smelling it and touching it, and watching it be touched by many hands as it passed down the line. But there were quite a number of hungry people who fell on the cake racks at tea breaks, who ate the cake instead of lunch, and illegally smuggled cake out in their handbags. That seemed to me to be the ultimate degradation.

Doreen was Irish, like quite a lot of the women. She had seven children. Her husband was working on a building site, but was often out of work. She was tiny, with a pinched face and red eyes. She had a cough that you could hear above the machines sometimes. She never talked unless someone spoke to her; saving up her energy, she would sit in a corner of the tea room smoking all through the breaks. She was one of the ones who ate cake at lunchtime and never went to the canteen. She looked about sixty, but was probably in her early forties. One tea break I sat next to her on the cramped benches in the tiny tea break room, with the floor covered by bits of cake and slopped tea, and the tea machine dripping, and no milk left. She said her husband disappeared from time to time, for as long as six months at once. When he was gone she couldn't afford to work, as the welfare paid her enough for her and her family to survive; she couldn't possibly earn a living wage on her own. The welfare refused to subsidise the women's wages, to bring them up to existence level, as that would encourage employers to pay less. 'If I didn't love the bugger,' she said, 'I'd say I was better off without him. I don't work for the love of it, I can tell you that. When he's away I get a rest.'

One afternoon as we came out of work – most of the girls looking immaculate with smart shoes and coats, hair perfectly set and not looking at all as if they'd just come out of that basement – I was walking down the street with Jenny, a West Indian woman of about forty. We were going in the same direction, and she asked me in for a cup of tea. She lived on the ground floor of a big crumbling Victorian house. The house was one of many in the area that were built for grander days, for families with servants, with big airy rooms. Structurally nothing much had been done to change it since then, so that on the ground floor she and her family were living in three rooms that had been grand and spacious dining and drawing rooms with high stuccoed ceilings and french windows. They had been partitioned with hardboard, and the walls papered cheaply, a long time ago. She had four children and they all had little windowless hardboard cubicles to sleep in. The paint was peeling from the damp, although it had obviously been painted quite recently. The bathroom was two floors up and shared by three families. There was very little furniture, and in the sitting room, which was also Jenny's and her husband's bedroom, they had improvised sofas with old car and bus seats along the wall, propped up on top of orange boxes. A woman in the basement looked after her two youngest children in the daytime, and we went down to collect them. There were eight children in the room. 'She's not a minder,' Jenny said. 'She just helps out. All the other mothers in the house work too.' Minder had become a dirty word to her. She'd left her children with minders before who didn't look after them at all well.

Jenny and her husband were paying thirteen pounds a week for the flat. He was earning nineteen pounds a week basic, so she had to work. She hated leaving her children, but she couldn't get them into a nursery.

Sally and Anne worked together. They always had done. They worked at one of the packing machines. They had both been there for three months. They both had blue-black hair, cut short in just the same way, and they wore the same shoes. They lived in the same street and their husbands drank together in the evenings. They were in their mid-twenties and were fairly typical of the mobile 30 per cent of the work force in the factory. They weren't going to stay much longer. Sally had found them jobs in a pen factory that paid more. They moved jobs quite often. 'We get bored otherwise,' Anne said. Her husband worked on the buses. She had a seven-year-old son at school and a younger daughter, whom she left with her sister all day. 'This is the worst job we've had in a long while,' Sally said. 'I don't know why we stuck it all this time.' The three of us used to have lunch together in the canteen. They worked, they both said, because they really needed the money. They both had mortgages to pay off. 'And another thing,' Sally said, 'you get bored with being married all the time, just being married. Anne and me worked together before we married, we were mates.' Anne laughed and said, 'It keeps us young.' They were strong and had almost limitless energy. They went out with their husbands most evenings, as well as looking after their children and working full-time. Somehow they kept going on their own incredible exuberance. 'Well, you can't rot, can you?' Sally said.

The factory employs several thousand people. There hasn't been a strike there since the general strike. The firm had in its early days gained a reputation for being good employers. As it grew much bigger, professional managers were employed, and the old paternalistic attitude disappeared. There wasn't a union, partly because they used to pay well above union rates. This is no longer the case. The wages are low for the area. The conditions are not particularly good and the canteen is not heavily subsidised. The new professional set of managers are more concerned with getting a higher 'through-put' per hour on the lines, with greater flexibility of labour and improved plant efficiency, than with having a contented work force.

In each department there is a person who is supposed to make suggestions for greater efficiency, and to take suggestions from the workers to the management.

When I left the factory, I went back to see an executive of the department I had worked in. I told him I had worked there incognito and that I was writing a book. His attitude was that I was one person who could help him out of his difficulties. He showed not the slightest apprehension.

His office was in the big administrative building in the centre of the compound, and his window looked out on to the works. He was a cheerful friendly man, and as I came into the room, he took out a pencil and notebook and said, 'I have a problem which I think you could help me with. We have great recruiting difficulties, and too many people are leaving. Why is it? Have you any suggestions?'

I suggested that higher wages might help.

He smiled and rubbed his hands and answered straight away, 'Of course we'd love to raise the wages, but the government won't let us.' Since then the wages have risen considerably. He explained the difficulties of getting higher productivity in many of the departments. 'There doesn't seem to be the right sort of feeling in the factory,' he said. 'Not much loyalty, not a strong enough sense of people identifying with the work and the firm. Perhaps if there were a union, they would feel more bound together and there wouldn't be such a quick turnover of labour. It would help people identify, perhaps.' He was worried, and the new recruiting programme was not as much of a help as he had hoped. 'And then there were a lot of redundancies when we closed one department down. I think that may have made people feel the work here wasn't too secure. Perhaps there were too many coloured people working here,' he said, looking around for a scapegoat. 60 per cent of the workers in the bakery are coloured.

He had a great many other problems, too. With overtime, half of the labour force were working a 50-hour week, but by law, men are restricted to twenty-six weeks a year on night work. He was having to employ men in women's jobs. 'Men aren't very good at things like rolling up Swiss rolls. The wastage rate shoots up when we have to put them on those jobs.' Also, for reasons of economy, some women were doing jobs that men used to do. 'But of course,' he said, 'they aren't allowed to lift more than twenty two pounds.'

The factory, built nearly 50 years ago, was out of date and insufficiently automated. He told me that a far greater percentage of the price of the cakes from that factory represented labour costs than was spent on labour in other factories owned by the firm, and that was nothing to do with the wages being higher. People were employed instead of machines.

The production manager had been with the firm a good many years, he didn't like to say how many. When he joined, there was a training scheme that meant he spent three years working on the factory floor in every department, and he was given a six-month trial. The jobs haven't changed much since then, so he knows all the processes pretty well, and he knows what it feels like. In many ways he's a very sympathetic man, but he has his job to do, with all its problems. 'For anyone with intelligence and drive, there are opportunities here,' he said. 'But a lot of people don't want promotion. Take old Rose in the tart department. She's a gorgon, and marvellous at her job, but she refuses to do any other work. We've tried to move her up but she won't.'

In fact, in the cake bakery there were 90 people working, and only two foreladies, both of whom had been there a great many years, so the chances of promotion are not very great. There are various higher gradings that give people greater responsibilities and qualify them for a few shillings more a week. In theory you can become a junior forelady in a year. 'It's a question of selling yourself, making yourself noticed, being an extrovert,' the manager explained. Quality inspectors get 10 per cent extra, and foreladies get between seventeen and twenty-two pounds a week. Promotion prospects didn't much interest the people I spoke to.

I shook hands with the manager and left as someone came in with the production figures of the month. He was pondering over the huge charts showing the theoretical throughput and the actual throughput and the wastage and the costs and the profits.

Chapter Three

# Maternity Ward

It was six forty-five in the morning and the Domestic Supervisor led me up three flights of stairs and into the kitchen where I was to work. I had a uniform with half the buttons missing, and a frayed threadbare cloak with St Mathilda's embroidered on it at one corner. 'This is your new ward orderly,' said the Supervisor to the Sister we met in the corridor. Sister glanced at me quickly, gave a very faint nod, and hurried on.

The kitchen was quite small, but light, in spite of the thick old frosted glass in the windows. If you pressed your nose against the panes you could just see that the room gave on to one of those dark wells to be found in the middle of a great many badly designed Victorian buildings. An auxiliary nurse was sitting slouched in the corner with her mouth full of bread. She was swallowing hard as we came in, and she stuffed the crusts into her pocket and leapt to her feet, afraid the Supervisor would see. 'Your new orderly,' the Supervisor said again, and the auxiliary gulped and smiled. 'You'll pick it up,' said the Supervisor and disappeared.

There was a huge fridge in the kitchen with a big notice in red on it; 'Blood must not be stored in this refrigerator under any circumstances whatsoever.' Inside there were rows and rows of milk bottles. There was an old gas stove at one end of the room, and a row of huge cooking pots at the other end, next to the sink. In a small cupboard were bottles of ketchup, cornflakes, Camp coffee and O.K. sauce. The floor was very old battered dark red lino, the kind that only looks passably clean when it's wet.

The auxiliary nurse smiled at me again when the Supervisor had gone, and she fished out the crusts of bread from her pocket, and began eating them again. She was a tall ill-looking Swedish girl with red eyes and acne. She was always tired and hungry, although she ate a great deal. 'You're lucky to be in this ward,' she said. 'There's no disease here.' A couple of babies down the passage were yowling wretchedly. 'You know there have been six different orderlies up here in the last two months?' Why? 'Either they left because they couldn't stand hospital work, or else they were moved to somewhere not so nice so that a new one could come up here. They try not to give the new ones the worst wards because they wouldn't stay.'

A sharp voice in the distance shouted out 'Auxiliary!, Auxiliary!' and she shot to her feet and hurried off to sterilize more babies' bottles. A small Irish nurse came bristling into the kitchen, 'Orderly? Where's the breakfast?' she demanded. She put her hands firmly on to her hips and stared at me. She turned and marched out of the room muttering 'Why do they always have to send the half wits to Ward 7D?'

I boiled up water for tea and put plates and cutlery on a trolley. I couldn't find any evidence of sugar, bread, or food, and was looking around when a tiny fat Indian girl came in and said she'd help me. I asked her where the food was kept. She threw her hands in the air and roared. She nipped about the kitchen producing things from the most unexpected places, a dusty plate of ready buttered bread from behind the stove, tea from behind the fridge, sugar from under the sink. 'You have to learn about that,' she said. 'It's the night nurses. They'll eat the whole lot if you don't hide it from them before you go home in the evening. Then there's nothing left for the patients because you can't get more than the ration.'

Outside the kitchen was an electric trolley, plugged into the wall and smelling of old grease. It had been there all night, simmering the breakfast in a sea of cooking oil. Inside there were shrivelled and saturated eggs and bacon, cooked by the evening shift of kitchen staff and sent round to the wards at nine the night before, and a congealed container of lumpy porridge. All the meals were cooked by the central kitchen and sent to the small kitchens in the wards in these electric trolleys.

We were late with the breakfast and the nurses were shouting. They were bullied by their superiors and so they bullied us in turn. There was a running battle between nurses and orderlies.

Ward 7D consisted of a main ward at the end of the passage, and two smaller side wards – an average of thirty patients. It was, I was assured over and over again, the nicest ward in the hospital. Mothers who had just had their babies were put into it, with the babies in cradles at the side of the bed.

It was seven o'clock. The Indian orderly and I wheeled the breakfast trolley into the ward and laid the table in the middle. The women were gazing at us blearily. Most would rather have had no breakfast than eat it at that hour. But the nurses bustled them out of bed. The mothers in the side wards were allowed to have theirs sitting in their chairs beside their beds. There was almost no talk at the table, and soon some of the babies began to howl and the nurses called to the women, 'Come along, Mrs Edwards. Don't take all day. Baby needs feeding as well, you know.' And the women got up from the table to deal with their babies.

The women looked miserable for most of the time. They were longing to get out. About half of them were having their first babies and all of them were young, in their twenties. The nurses were bossy and busy and had no time to make them happy. Their fourteen days in hospital was one long trial for them. They didn't talk much amongst themselves, and they tried to sleep away all the time that they were not tending to their babies. Many of them would lie for hours doing nothing at all.

'Come on, quick,' the other orderly was saying to me. 'Get it all cleared away quick.' So we packed everything on to the trolley and hurried back to the kitchen. 'Come on, come on!' she said, and picked up what was left of the bread and butter, sugar and cornflakes. At that moment three nurses came in. One was thin and dressed like a nun, two were fat Africans in blue uniforms. They descended on the trolley like vultures and grabbed as much of the bread as they could, sprinkled it with sugar, carefully divided the one remaining piece of bacon and ate that, took huge mugs of milk, knocked it back, and made off down the corridor because Sister was calling them. The orderly had said nothing all this time. We both just watched. 'That happens if you don't get it cleared away quick,' she said. 'Now we'll be short of bread and butter for dinner.' She hid what was left behind the stove again, and put the sugar in the oven. 'Why didn't you stop them?' 'If it was for the patients, they shouldn't go eating it all,' I said lamely. The girl rolled up her sleeves ready for the washing up. 'Oh, don't try making trouble with the nurses,' she said. 'It's not worth it.' We washed up the breakfast.

Then we cleaned the kitchen. It was the sort of cleaning that in fact leaves everything pretty dirty. The kitchen was old, the lino on the floor battered and the paint on the walls faded so that it couldn't be made clean. There were decades of dirt under and around the stove, in corners, round the dustbins and the sink. We washed the floor, wiped the table, the stove and the fridge, cleaned surfaces and everything immediately visible, and although this was done every day, there was an indelible atmosphere of ingrained dirt in the place.

'Time for coffee,' said the orderly. I poured several pints of milk into a huge saucepan and set out cups on the trolley, pouring a minute drop of Camp coffee into each cup. The bottle of coffee had to be made to last. We wheeled the coffee round the ward and the women complained about it, but drank it out of boredom.

When the cups and saucers were washed up, it was time to clean the wards and the bathrooms and lavatories. In the wards we emptied water-jugs on the side tables, cleaned the tops, rearranged the get-well cards and the congratulations cards and the Lucozade bottles.

Dinner time was twelve o'clock and we would set the table, and wheel in the big electric trolley that had been sent up from the kitchens. Sister had caught on to the fact that food disappeared mysteriously, and insisted on dishing up the dinner and the supper herself. But often the nurses were too quick for her. They would watch for the arrival of the trolley, grab a plate, fill it up, and hide it in the cupboard until after the meal and then come in and eat it. This meant that sometimes there wasn't enough to go round, and I would be sent down to the kitchen by Sister to complain and demand more. The people in the kitchen would fly into a rage and shout and yell and accuse me of stealing it, but they scraped together a helping or two to take back to the ward.

School meals, canteen meals, greasy road-side café meals were three star luxuries compared to the stuff that was dished up in this hospital. The mince was thin and grey, more like soup. Several times a week there would be a slimy cheese custard that slithered around on the plate in a sea of water and tasted of flour and egg powder. Rice pudding, sago and tapioca were the only puddings, except on Sunday when there was a teaspoonful of ice cream and a thimbleful of jelly. Otherwise there were indeterminate greens and grisly stews, cheese flans that were all uncooked flan and no cheese, and sometimes on better days, tiny shrivelled chops which had been cooked so long that the fat had gone hard and the one square inch of meat had turned to shredded leather. The patients ate as little as they could and complained to the orderlies all the time, but when they were hungry, they ate it. Many of them had visitors who brought them sandwiches to keep them going.

After washing up lunch, the orderlies from each ward would queue up to collect the next day's ration from the store cupboard downstairs. The food was issued by a Sister who kept a strict count on exactly how much went to each ward, and there was no way of getting more than your small share – three sliced loaves, a dollop of butter and a bigger dollop of marge, some sugar poured into your tin, a bit of tea and cornflakes. A bottle of Camp coffee, a small dollop of marmalade (which rarely reached the patients), and eggs for boiling for Sunday breakfast when the kitchen staff were off. Milk was delivered to the ward and there was plenty.

We took back the rations and hid them, and then buttered the bread for the next day, as this was the only time we had for doing it. We melted up the butter and marge so as to make sure we could spread it thinly enough to cover all three sliced loaves. That meant spreading it so thin that you could hardly see it was there at all, and by the next morning the ready buttered bread had gone dry and it curled at the edges. Everything in the hospital was done by strict routine, including the orderlies' job, and the bread was always buttered after lunch.

The orderlies were treated with utter contempt. We were not the very bottom of the lines – the cleaners who mopped the corridors and wards were the lowest. Most of the orderlies were Maltese, Indian, Portuguese, or Irish. We worked a basic forty hour week, plus compulsory overtime Saturdays and Sundays. The shifts operated on a rota system, six forty-five in the morning to one o'clock in the afternoon, ten o'clock in the morning until four, three o'clock until nine in the evening. This meant you were alone on the breakfast shift, but worked with another orderly over lunch, and were alone again on the evening shift. As there were never enough orderlies to operate the system, the rota was erratic and one might do a double shift, or be working alone when you were scheduled to have someone helping. The basic pay was £12.70 a week and for the hours and the shifts, that was not good money. It was hard work, in that there was never time to stop, but once you learnt where everything was and what time each job had to be done, it was not difficult. The orderlies were on the whole much nicer than the nurses, and they probably worked less hard, having no night duties. They were a rowdy, jolly group of women, many not speaking a word of English. Many spoke their own language all the time. They tried to work together in their ethnic groups, so that they could speak to each other. They were friendly and resilient. They didn't like the work, or the nurses, and their main pre-occupation was keeping themselves out of trouble.

I thought it a dreadful job, in that it was regimented down to the last detail, and we were shouted at all the time by tired cross people. Most of the orderlies not being English nationals had to work in hospitals if they wanted to stay in England. If that system was changed, the government might have to resort to other compulsory labour to get people to take these jobs.

Working at St Mathilda's as an orderly gave me a worm's eye view of what hospital means for the working class. I was not in a position to see some of the most important aspects of the hospital life – orderlies are kept out of sight when the doctors make their rounds and I never saw one. Nor could I observe the work of the almoner or the influence of the matron. But I saw a great deal of the nurses and the patients.

All the patients were working class although the hospital bordered on middle class territory. It was the sort of hospital where middle class people would only find themselves if they were taken there unconscious. If they have any choice in the matter they set about getting themselves into one of the teaching hospitals. They wouldn't have a baby in a hospital like that. These places are for those who don't know the difference between one hospital and another, and so find themselves in understaffed over-worked impoverished local ones.

Of the thirty patients in the ward, about eight were coloured, and one or two of those hardly spoke any English at all. The nurses never had time to stop and explain or to sit and talk to any of them. There were no radios in the ward. The women sat in bed most of the day doing nothing. Sometimes they would glance at an occasional magazine, mostly they would lie there. Sometimes they would take down their cards and look at them again. Otherwise they would wait for visiting time at four o'clock. There was a television room down the passage, but television doesn't really get going until about seven o'clock, and by the time they had had supper, they had bored themselves into a state of exhaustion and they crept back into bed to sleep a good twelve hours. In the mornings when we cleaned the wards we saw most of the patients and were able to talk to them a little.

On the first day that I was there, a woman was brought in and put into a bed in a small partitioned-off space at the end of the ward. She was hugely fat, in her mid twenties, with lank ginger hair and freckles. All day she lay there heaving and crying and moaning, and refusing to eat or drink anything. Sometimes she slept, but was awoken by the howling of the babies, and then began to cry again herself. She had just lost her baby and couldn't bear the sounds of all the babies in the ward. It seemed such cruelty to put her into this ward, and not into a general gynaecological ward. 'Come on, pull yourself together!' 'Now stop all this moping,' the nurses would say to her as they passed her bed, but they didn't stop to talk or comfort her. Eventually one or two of the other patients came into her little section of the ward and began to chat to her; they persuaded her to come and sit at the table, and slowly she got happier. But as she began to reveal herself, the other patients retreated in horror. She would tell appalling stories across the table, and she shocked most of them. First of all she admitted openly that her husband was in prison and her other three children were in care. As she lumbered across the room to sit down, the other patients began to move away. Her one topic of conversation was her dead baby, but they listened with horrified fascination.

'My fella was there when it was born,' she'd say. 'Well it went on and on and on for hours and I was yelling and screaming. Then they told him to go out of the room when it was coming and he saw it. Well, he said he couldn't quite see it, but he just got a glimpse. He says it was horrible. You see, I reckon the head came out separately. I could feel it. I think the head came right off. There was blood everywhere.' And every day the story got more grotesque. 'I reckon it wasn't even human. It was all for the best.'

The nurses were a mixed group. They came and went week by week, and in this ward, only half of them actually belonged to the hospital. The rest were free-lance agency nurses, who, like temporary secretaries, could make more money by being hired out to hospitals by the week, than by being attached to any one place. In between hospital work, they would try and get more lucrative jobs as private nurses. This only happens in the poor hospitals where no one wants to go. In the big teaching hospitals all the nurses actually belong. You could tell the agency nurses apart as they all wore different uniforms, the uniforms of the hospitals they had originally trained at. They held themselves apart from the others, thinking themselves a superior breed. Almost all the resident nurses were Irish or black. Apart from Sister, only one nurse in the ward was white and English.

The permanent nurses were the most miserable and down-trodden. And the more down-trodden they were, the worse they treated the patients. There was always a shortage of them in the ward, and they worked extremely hard. There wasn't time for them to think much about the patients as people, even if they had had the energy and encouragement to do so. They shouted and quarrelled and bustled around, and sat down whenever the Sister's eye wasn't on them. The uniforms of the resident nurses were old and frayed although clean, and it was hard to see why they went on with the job at all. They worked very hard for no visible reward. The status outside the hospital of being a qualified nurse may have kept them going a bit, but they weren't out of the hospital very much. The romantic vision of '*Dr Kildare*' or '*Emergency Ward 10*' had nothing much to do with life at St Mathilda's.

The nurses didn't have time to pay much attention to babies. There was no cooing and chuckling at the tiny faces in the cradles. They carried them around like bundles. There was also little time to teach the new mothers how to look after them. Many of the young mothers were terrified of dealing with their babies, as no-one had shown them how. If they asked a busy nurse some simple question, they were quite likely to be told off. The mothers worried about whether their babies were eating too fast or too slow, whether they were sleeping enough, whether their heads were crooked, or their eyes were all right, or if there wasn't something a bit wrong with their bandy legs. But they had to sort their worries out amongst themselves, asking each other's advice, and hoping for the best. This meant that although they were longing to get out of hospital, they were also afraid that they wouldn't be able to deal with the babies alone, or that there might be something wrong with the baby which the nurses hadn't noticed.

In one of the side wards were two very weak babies who hardly ate at all and looked punier and more helpless than the others. They cried all day, and the mothers were miserable. The doctors were keeping an eye on them, and they would both be sent off for examinations and X-rays from time to time. The nurses were particularly irritated by one of these mothers. 'She fusses all day long,' one nurse said. 'Not surprising the baby cries. She gives us so much trouble that woman. Always complaining and asking for things. Expects to be treated different to all the others, a real little madam.' Said another, 'That baby won't last, I shouldn't think. Looks a goner to me.' I don't know whether the baby did live. The mother was let out and the baby went to a children's ward. To be a nurse at St Mathilda's you probably *had* to be as uninvolved with the patients as possible, just to survive and to get the work done.

The sisters were tough, kindly, but too busy to supervise everything. They bullied the nurses, but also knew how difficult it was for them when the hospital was under-staffed.

The only time I heard a couple of nurses talk to the patients other than to give them orders, was when they would sit down at the table with them after supper and tell them a series of the most hair-raising stories about babies and children with terrible deformities, or diseases that babies could have without anyone knowing. They would also give a running commentary on the accident cases that had come into Casualty that day. 'There was a little girl,' one would say. 'She can only have been about three, and she was run down by a bus. You should have seen her head. It was crushed so you'd think a steam roller had been over it.' And the patients listened, those are the sort of stories one doesn't want to hear but can't help listening to.

The nurses at St Mathilda's were over-worked. The management had no money. The Government had many priorities. And the patients were poor and unaware that better was to be had from grander hospitals.

Poverty goes further than lack of money. The poor are deprived in so many ways. They have worse education, are more ignorant, and will always get the worst of everything, from consumer goods to social services. From expensive shoddy furniture to impoverished and run-down hospitals.

Chapter Four

# Car Parts

'C' entrance looked more of a loading base for goods than a door for people. In the early morning we all rushed through the gap where they had opened some great metal shutters, and hurried in down a wide concrete-floored corridor. As we bustled down the passageway, everyone said 'Good morning' to everyone else; 'Terrible morning, isn't it?' Lining the passage were huge metal trucks full of different shaped mouldings, spare parts, crates of odd shaped metal pieces waiting to be worked on or waiting to be collected. High up on the brick walls, painted institutional cream and dark grey, there were large yellow printed notices of old factory acts, the laws about the proper use of power presses, the laws about industrial disease, information about dermatitis, and more factory acts in tiny print, dating back to the twenties. Down the long corridor there were several clocks, one for each shop. Ours was at the end and we had until three minutes past eight to clock in.

At first I hadn't noticed that the shop in which we were working had no windows. When the bus stopped outside the factory, Lucas's was just one factory among a whole long row spread down an arterial road out of the city. It looked the same as all the others – huge, square, and very functional. The red brick, in spite of regular cleaning, was dark with years of Brum smoke, and the dazzling neon Lucas sign jarred at that hour of the morning.

Almost every British car has a starting mechanism made by Lucas, so that if work stops at Lucas, then work stops in almost the entire industry, and the economy depends more on the car industry than on any one other. That means that the workers there could be said to be one of the strongest forces in the running of the country – in a week or two they could set the economy back by millions of pounds. They are in an almost unique position of power, but the power they hold is no more, in real terms, than that of a man with a machine gun; he can shoot down everyone in sight, the whole population if he likes, but it won't put his grievances right and it won't get him what he wants.

In Birmingham there are eleven Lucas plants. The pay was not as good as that of the car assembly workers and in comparison with them, it was generally considered that the women at Lucas were better paid than the men. In the car industry as a whole women's average earnings are £13.85 a week. Compared, say, to the bakery where I worked, the conditions were luxurious, the work fairly undemanding, the employers concerned, and the foremen friendly and gentle. As factories go, it was a good one, but as factories are terrible and deadening places to work in, so was this.

The top deck of the bus had been stuffy, smelling of stale smoke like the morning after a bottle party. But it was cold. The white men wore cloth caps, the black men, pork pies. At night the street lights in Birmingham give off a lunar gloom; in the morning as the daylight comes up, sodium is a sort of luxury.

The clock makes a loud ting as you slip your card into the slot and pull down the lever which punches the time on it. 'Talk about a one-armed bandit,' someone jokes as he presses down the lever. 'Trouble is, it's never been known to pay out.'

It was the others who kept pointing out that the shop had no windows. This was the finishing shop on the ground floor. We were making odds and ends for the other departments, electrical bits of all sorts, and cutting and preparing cables. I was written down as 'Switch Cable Operator', although for most of the time I was working on small bulb holders. It was difficult to find out exactly what was being made, because very few people knew quite what they were working on. Some of them had been on the same job for years and had never known what their particular bits were used for. They could have been anything from dynamos to detonators. Even the charge-hands often didn't know.

The finishing shop was a huge room with six or seven long benches, dividing the space into sections spread far apart to allow the men with electric fork lift trolleys to wheel their loads up and down. The noise level was reasonable and you could almost always hear what people were saying, apart from occasional ear-bursting explosions from a compressed air machine in the corner of the room. There were about thirty-five women and ten men working in the shop. In one corner, partly sealed off by a glass partition, was a large middle-aged woman who worked all day every day on her own. She was lacquering casings and baking them in an enormous furnace. She worked very hard, rarely spoke to anyone and, while I was there, she was stood over by the foreman for the whole of one week as he was trying to get 30,000 casings through a day. In another partitioned section was the paint shop, where a girl called Carla worked, spraying different parts that were sent down to her from the rest of the factory. Sometimes the paint or the work ran out and she came to work with me.

The atmosphere was relaxed, with no conveyor belts and only half the people on piecework. The foreman and the two charge hands never fussed if someone went over to chat with someone else for a few minutes. They seemed hand-picked for their air of benevolence and Dixon-of-Dock-Green chumminess. No one was timing how long you spent in the lavatory, either, as they do in plenty of other factories. In fact, in the first two hours I worked there, no fewer than six friendly women asked if I wanted to go to the lavatory. Eventually I agreed and Carla and I went into the big pink-tiled spotless cloakroom and found dozens of jolly women smoking and laughing. It was as smart as a grand hotel, with a row of electric hand-driers and scented liquid soap from silver taps above the sinks. On one wall was a row of mirrors. It was a strange contrast to the grim factory: a small pink oasis in a desert of cables, casings, trolleys, crates and machines.

Almost all the women working there had been at Lucas's for a good many years. The average age in this shop was about forty-five to fifty, and the turnover of labour on the day shift was very low. Some of the older ones had been working there together for twenty-five or thirty years. Many of the women were working, not really out of necessity, but for luxuries. A great many came to work in cars, and had a family income of as much as forty pounds a week. Birmingham is a rich city and the car industry is full of the much written about 'affluent workers'. Outside the factory was a butcher's shop used by the women in the surrounding factories who do their shopping in the dinner break. A butcher's shop is a good test of the affluence of an area. In the window were vast joints, expensive steaks, lush chops and choice cuts – none of those grisly indeterminate innards, gizzards, guts and scrag ends, the inescapable sign of deprivation and poverty.

Work in the finishing shop was fairly unrepresentative of the jobs in the rest of the factory. We were only doing small orders, where any single line didn't last long. This meant that people tended to be moved around from one job to another, which was very rare in the departments that had been making the same component for years. The jobs didn't in themselves vary much; there can't have been more than six basic processes going on. Most of the women resented being moved around. 'All the jobs are boring,' one woman explained, 'so it's better to stay on the one you know and don't have to think about any more.' There were some shops where the workers were especially picked, after manual dexterity tests, chosen for their ability and constantly moved. The personnel manager said that those people were often discontented. This was partly due to the fact that when they were moved from one piecework job to another, it took some time for them to acquire the skill to get the full piecework rate, and for a few weeks they would lose some of their piecework bonus. It wasn't only the monotony of doing one job for years, it was also the fact that every job in itself was monotonous that made life in the factory so dreary. In the end, apparent variety of jobs doesn't make much difference.

The bulb holders I was working on took three stages to make. First there was a pile of short cables from which I had to cut the plastic away from the wire at either end. To do this I had a small cutting machine with a foot pedal: It was very hot, to cut the plastic more easily. It required efficient co-ordination between hands and feet. You had to press the pedal to bring down the blade when exactly the right length of cable was underneath and your fingers were out of the way. If you touched any part of the machine it burnt you: I burnt myself several times at first. It was simple enough, but anything repeated that many times can get confusing. The second stage was to thread the two cables into a rubber holder, like threading two needles at once. The third stage was to fix metal clips on to the ends of the wires, and this needed the most concentration. The clips were in a machine in a long line. You put the wire into the machine carefully, with your fingers, and when it was in the right place you pulled on a big wheel and a heavy press hurtled down and stamped the clip shut. It meant working for most of the time with one hand under the press and one hand on the wheel that brought the press down. It's easy to get mesmerized and quite often as I brought the press down with a great thud, I wondered for a split second whether my hand was still underneath. But there were few accidents, and if you are working at your own speed, being careful, I suppose it is not particularly dangerous. My job was reasonably varied – it had three stages – but even so, the day was very long.

Dulcie worked harder than anyone else in the shop. She was cutting cables on piecework and all day long she worked ferociously, uninterrupted by anything except the breaks. Her face was completely expressionless, her eyes almost glazed over, her hands moving with incredible speed as she operated the cutter with a foot pedal. The noise of her cutter was the most regular sound in the shop.

One week there were no cables for her to cut, so she was sent over to work with me on the bulb holders. She grumbled a great deal about being taken off her piecework job and being put back to a make-up rate, so that she lost about 70 pence a day. I thought she would have been pleased to get the rest, to get away from the terrible speed at which she had been working, but she wasn't.

For three days we worked together, and she told me about her life.

Dulcie was born in a small town outside Leeds in 1909. She was one of a large family, and was set to work in the mills as soon as she was thirteen. She hardly went to school and only learnt to read and write properly after she was married. 'Education, that's what I miss!' she says. 'If I'd had education my life would have been different, I'm sure of that.' At seventeen she got married, in spite of her family's disapproval. Her husband, Reg, is seventeen years older than her. He was then the manager of a small grocer's shop. They lived for a time very happily, and she went to work with him in the shop. Then the depression came. The grocer's shop was closed down, and neither of them could get a job. They were both on the dole for a year, so they decided to come South to look for work. 'It was a toss-up between Birmingham and London,' Dulcie said, and laughed. 'Reg took up a coin and tossed. Birmingham was heads and heads won.' When they reached Birmingham, they took a small cold room in a lodging house. 'There were rats and cockroaches and no one was friendly to us. I hated Birmingham.' But after four months they both found jobs. 'I can tell you, when you've been on the Labour for a year, you'll take anything. Reg went for a job at Lucas's. He'd have done almost anything before going into a factory, but that's all there was. When he went for the job he said he was a skilled pipe fitter, and that he'd done factory work all his life. Well, they couldn't tell by looking at his hands, seeing he'd been out of work all that time. They believed him and they gave him the job. The first month he was there he had a hard time, having to make out he knew it all. He used to write down what he had to do on his hand, so as not to forget. One day the gaffer saw him doing that and he said, 'You've not worked in a factory before, have you?' Reg had to admit it, but they kept him on all the same, because he was such a good worker. He stayed there till he retired at sixty-eight.

Dulcie's first job in Birmingham was in a factory doing light engineering. 'In those days,' she says, 'women did heavier work. I was lucky to get a job on lacquering. It was messy, but not too hard.' When she had been there two years, the boss moved her on to a very heavy job, working with heavy chains, and he moved his niece into her job. 'I shouted at him for that. He sacked me on the spot. Well, when you're young, you don't think about consequences. I must have been mad to take a risk like that, when jobs were so hard to come by.' But she got a job soon afterwards, with her husband at Lucas, well over thirty years ago. 'Apart from that year on the Labour, and the times I've been in hospital, there hasn't been a time in my life since I was twelve when I wasn't working,' she said, with a mixture of pride and regret. 'When I come to think of it, I've worked myself to the bone all these years, and all for what?'

They moved to a small house a long way from work. They had to travel two hours a day. Later they were offered a council house nearer the centre of Birmingham. It was in very bad condition, but they were delighted to get it, although the roof leaked and they hadn't much money for putting it right.

It took a long time for her to get used to Birmingham. For the first ten years she used to go back to Leeds whenever she could. 'I was slow finding friends,' she says. 'I don't bother with many people now. You see when you haven't got a family in a place, and when you move around so you don't have many neighbours, you don't have too many friends. It doesn't worry me. I don't want to be bothered with many people.'

Ten years ago the council moved them out of their house, as they hadn't any children, to give the house to a family of four. Dulcie and Reg were moved to a part of Birmingham half an hour's journey from work. They live in a small prefab with a garden. They liked it there very much, although they didn't like being moved away from the only people in Birmingham they knew. But two years ago the M6 motorway began to be built and it came right to their back garden, cutting off a bit of it. 'The noise is dreadful and they left a terrible mess all over the place. Our garden is all filled with tar. The council won't move us and of course, it being a council house, you don't get any compensation or anything.'

Reg is now seventy-seven, and he has been retired for nearly ten years. All the time Dulcie was talking she was working very fast, fitting the wires into the rubber bulb holders.

Reg worked at Lucas as a welder. A few years before he was due to retire, he lost an eye when a piece of red-hot metal flew into it. 'He had this accident, and his eye was very sore for a week, but he didn't think too much of it. Then at the weekend, we were out shopping, and suddenly he says "I can't see out of my eye." We thought it would pass off, but when we got home he still couldn't see. We went to the hospital and they said he wouldn't see with it again. They said if he'd gone for treatment straight away they might have saved it. Of course we did think of claiming compensation from Lucas, but Reg was scared he'd lose his job if he did. And if you get sacked before you actually retire, you lose most of your pension. So we thought it better to leave it at that.' He would not, in fact, have lost his job. He might probably have received some sort of payment.

A year ago Dulcie had a serious nervous breakdown and she was off work for six months. 'It was the work that did it,' she thinks. 'I was working on components that had twenty-eight parts. It was piecework and you couldn't stop for a moment if you wanted to get your time in. You know, I looked a lot better before that breakdown. People used to say I couldn't be a day over forty. But since then, well, I know I'm not what I was. It makes you think. It made me think about lots of things. Well, I haven't had a bad life when you come to think. If we'd gone to London we wouldn't have ended up in factory work. We might have had a little shop or something. And I don't think I'd have worked so hard. It doesn't seem worth it, does it? But I can't complain, really. You live your life and you get what's coming to you, don't you?'

When Dulcie retires she and Reg are going to live during the summer months in a caravan in Skegness, where she will work part-time at Butlins as a lavatory cleaner, mornings only, eight to eleven, for £4.50 a week. She will get about five pounds old age pension. After working for Lucas for nearly thirty years, she will get a pension (non-contributory) from them of about two pounds a week, and both she and Reg will get a Christmas hamper every year. In the winter they will go back to their prefab in Birmingham. All the same, she was looking forward to her retirement.

After three days a new supply of cables was sent down to be cut. Dulcie was put back on her machine and I didn't see very much of her after that. Friendships in factories are rather arbitrary affairs. That may be why people don't see each other outside work. They resent the work, and so they resent being forced into friendships with people they haven't chosen for themselves. When nearly everyone I met said, 'Oh no, I wouldn't mix with this lot outside work,' I felt it was an expression of dislike of the work situation rather than any genuine feeling of their superiority over the other workers.

Carla was young. She worked in the paint-shop next door, almost entirely on her own. She was by far the youngest of the women I worked with, and I got to know her better than any of the others. We spent our breaks together, and when the supply of paint ran out she always came to talk to me. We made friends just after Dulcie had told me her story. It coloured my picture of Carla and her life. I couldn't help feeling that Carla was just at the beginning of the life that Dulcie was ending, although she talked about it in quite a different way. She didn't see her life or her work with the kind of clarity that looking back over sixty years gave Dulcie. To Carla, her job was just a job she happened to be doing, not a way of life for the next thirty-five years.

Carla was married last year to Will, in a Catholic church, in white, and they have a house of their own which they'll finish paying for in twenty-five years' time. He earns on average twenty-five pounds a week, and she earns about fifteen pounds. They pay ten pounds a week to a firm called 'Secure Homes' which pays their mortgage, gas and electricity bills. They have a second-hand car, and have decided not to have children for another two years, until they've got fitted carpets and a few other things for the house. 'I'd like to have four children,' she says, 'but we'll only be able to afford two.'

Carla intends to go on working for most of her life. 'I'll stop till the kids get to school age. But we could always do with the money. Will doesn't earn that much. The thing is, keep moving jobs. I won't stay here too long, I shouldn't think. Except of course it's very convenient, with Will working here too, and us coming in to work by car.' I don't think she was very convinced by the thought that she might change jobs. It didn't matter to her all that much. She thought mostly about her home, and didn't think about her work. She didn't let it dominate her life. But then, she was still young, and for Dulcie working life looked rather different.

After I had been at Lucas's for a while, there was a strike. There hadn't been one in that factory for as long as most people could remember. The rumours began on the Friday and the atmosphere in the finishing shop changed abruptly. First there was excitement, tension, eagerness, political discussion by the women that I hadn't heard before either at Lucas's or anywhere else. Later the excitement changed to concern, and the place was bristling with conflicting emotions.

The foreman and the charge hands were going on strike for seven pounds and five pounds more a week. They wanted to restore the differential between themselves and the workers they supervised. There were some shops where the charge hands were getting less money than some of the workers. Over the last few years a number of wage claims had gone through for the workers, and the foremen's and charge hands' pay hadn't risen correspondingly. The strikers were members of A.S.T.M.S., a branch of which union had only quite recently formed in the factory. Some of the charge hands and foremen weren't members, and still belonged to Transport and General Workers' Union, which did not join in, so some of the shops continued to work as usual.

Six hundred supervisors came out on Monday from three of the Lucas factories. It was reported in the newspapers that on the second day 19,000 workers in the car industry were laid off as a result of the strike.

The foremen and charge hands, the supervisors, are always in a difficult position. Technically they belong to the management, but emotionally they feel themselves to be workers, having spent most of their lives as ordinary working men. They act as the buffers for the management, and because they have to some extent defected from the workers, a great deal of often unjustified venom is levelled at the best of them. They are constantly watched for 'putting on airs' and for any trace of officiousness or self-importance.

The foreman of the finishing shop was a tall, beaming man who seemed kind and jolly, like a cheerful village policeman. He was responsible for all work in the shop. At first I thought he was liked by everyone, and it was only after a while that I noticed the resentment and distrust people felt towards him. 'The gaffer's as two-faced as the devil himself,' Dulcie would say at every opportunity.

There was one woman who had to fit the ends of the cables that Dulcie cut into slots in small boxes. If the cables were a little short, her job was more difficult. She was hated by everyone else in the shop, except a huge and mountainous woman, for whom she brought cakes and pies every day, 'to buy her friendship,' as Dulcie said. Whenever the gaffer came by her, she would ostentatiously be measuring up the cables and holding up the short ones so that he couldn't fail to see them. He would then stop and examine them, and go and tell off Dulcie or whoever was responsible. Dulcie would go quite white with rage when he approached her and although she was never actually rude, she used to spit back her answers at him. 'There isn't another gaffer in the place that would listen to tell-tales. It makes nothing but trouble. That woman was sent down here because the gaffer upstairs wouldn't have her. He said she was a troublemaker,' Dulcie said. 'Our gaffer listens to any tale anyone cares to tell.' Later I was sent to work with the woman who told tales, and I understood why she did it. If the cables were short, her job took twice as long to do and she lost half her piecework time. If she pointed out to the 'gaffer' that she couldn't possibly get them done because of the defect, he would make up her time on the books and she got her full money. Her job was a very fiddly one anyway, and even on good days she had to work at breakneck speed to get enough done, as it was valued badly. This is the sort of situation where whatever he did, the gaffer couldn't do right.

But he did tend to be a little condescending. He would come up to people at work with a royal grin and say, 'Everything all right then?' and they would smile and nod back to him. But when he turned his back, they made faces. When something went wrong in the shop, when a batch of cables was returned, or he had a complaint from high up about productivity, he would stomp up and down looking black and picking on people, trying to pass the buck down the line, even when the fault was in the specification or the interpretation of it. But I liked him.

He seemed to be under constant pressure, imagined or real, and he had a kind of stature and firmness.

One social distinction between the gaffer and the charge hands was that he wore a suit every day and they wore overalls. It was purely a question of status; the gaffer was in the shop all day and was often seen to use his hands. Incidentally, the overall, or rather the no overall, was a universal status symbol in the factory. Nearly a third of the people working there were in the offices, on the administrative side, and at work they didn't mix with the factory hands. There was a cloakroom labelled Staff Ladies, which Carla and I used to go into because it was nearest the shop. It was always full of secretaries and they made a great point of not speaking to us, because we were in overalls and belonged to the shop floor. Another distinction between the gaffer and the two charge hands was that he was called Mr Taylor and they were called Norman and Bill.

Norman was a tall, dark, pale man who worked very hard, was never flustered, never told anyone off. He was respected, and went out of his way to keep as quiet as he could and to be noticed by no one. If something went wrong, he put it right. He was uncritical and scrupulously sensitive about the embarrassments of his job.

Bill was the other charge hand. 'He's past it,' they all said, and most disregarded him as a doddery old fool. But in some ways he was sharper than Norman and the gaffer. He was less involved with the work and the factory than they, but more interested in the general implications of his life there. He talked about unionism, the Labour party, foreign affairs and his forty years at Lucas's.

Of the three of them, Bill had been the only one to join the Lucas branch of A.S.T.M.S. when it started up. The others had stayed in the T.G.W.U. although it could not represent them so well. As a result, only Bill went out on strike.

The strike quickly separated out the poor from the reasonably well-off women in the shop. When on Monday morning all the workers in the factory were kept on as usual, no one took the strike very seriously. The richer ones were laughing and saying to each other 'I could just do with a few days off work.' But by the afternoon some of the shops upstairs were closed where all the supervisors were, and the workers were laid off by the firm. Having nothing to do, they drifted into our shop, some of them laughing still, most of them worried. There was a mild feeling of panic. It hadn't happened before and no one had really thought they might be laid off. Some of the papers and the television reports had predicted that it might last weeks, or even months. Everyone was faced with the prospect that next week they might all be signing on at the Labour exchange, and the dole was something that all the older ones were horrified by, remembering the thirties. There were rumours that when we came in to work the next day, we too would be laid off. One woman with no husband and a number of children said that if it happened she would have to leave at once and find another job. A few of the others were in the same position.

Feelings about the strike were mixed. 'Of course, they're right to strike,' said one woman. 'How can a charge hand earn less than the men he oversees?' 'They're quite right,' said another, 'but fancy asking for another seven pounds a week. They've got a nerve. It's more than half what I get as it is.' One of the worse off women said, 'Whatever the rights and wrongs of it, I don't think they should cause so much suffering, getting 19,000 laid off. It's not fair on the others.' 'Anyway,' said someone else, 'it's a gaffers' strike and who cares about the gaffers? It's us that get it, not them.' But although there was bewilderment and some indignation at the supervisors' action, there was also a feeling that when it came to the point, the strikers were right – all strikes are good strikes, that showed that the supervisors were really workers and not management. If any person from the management proper had walked into the shop and asked them what they thought about the strike, all the workers would have supported it, and their criticisms of it they would have kept to themselves.

That day the gaffer and Norman, who weren't out on strike, were almost put in Coventry. Everyone muttered audibly about them when they came past. 'It isn't right,' Dulcie said loudly as the gaffer was standing a little way from where we were working. 'If the strike wins it's all the supervisors that'll get the benefit, not just those on strike. The gaffer and Norman go on getting their pay while the others are out, and getting no money. They should be out there too.' Technically neither Mr Taylor nor Norman were strike breaking. They belonged to another union although some non-A.S.T.M.S. members were out. But all the same, they were glowered at and despised and regarded as blacklegs of the first order.

As the strike wore into the second and third day, our shop was one of those still functioning. There was quite a backlog of work to be got through, so we were not immediately dependent on the shops that had closed down. While criticism of the strikers got stronger, so did a general feeling of discontent with the management. Everything was thrown into the melting pot, and I heard people voicing all kinds of complaints I hadn't heard before. Parity with the rest of the motor industry was demanded. The whole question was argued of whether a firm had the right not to pay its workers when they are laid off, without any pay, as a result of a strike that was nothing to do with them. Why should a firm be allowed to hold one group of workers responsible for the action of another group, sometimes in a different firm altogether? If there were a strike, wasn't that the firm's problem, and not the other workers'?

One dinner time in the canteen I sat next to a man who was talking very articulately about unofficial strikes. 'The unions,' he said, 'have lost all contact with the workers. There have to be unofficial strikes if the unions won't sanction any strikes at all. People assume from the way that the papers write it, that strikes are a sort of luxury, a holiday that the wicked workers indulge in from time to time. They forget that it's us that suffer twice as much as the country does. I mean, when we go out on strike, it's us that goes on the dole, falls behind with HP payments, the rent and God knows what else. Now the country may suffer a serious setback, and of course strikes are a bad thing for the economy, but don't let anyone think we do it for fun. And if the strike's unofficial, we don't get any strike-pay either. Now the very fact that there are so many unofficial strikes is proof that unions no longer represent their members.'

He then made a point that seemed to me more important than

anything I have ever heard or seen written recently about strikes. When a Labour government is in power, he said, it is more or less inevitable that there should be a tremendous rise in the number of unofficial strikes. If the government in power were Conservative, there would probably be the same number of strikes, or more, but more of them would be sanctioned by the unions. With Labour in power the unions to some extent become too identified with the government and the economic interests of the country. The very nature of a trade union is anti-government. It exists to protect the workers from the forces of management, and to protect them from the economic planners, whose aim is to make the country richer, to bake a bigger cake, but to go on giving everyone the same slice. In fact, most of the time the unions are there to ensure that the workers go on getting the same slice, to ensure that their wages keep up with the standard of living. There are very few strikes that are actually demanding more. The Labour government's prices and incomes policy was a very good example. Wages were forcibly held down, which is reasonably easy for the government to control, and prices continued to rise, which is far more difficult for the government to check effectively. The Labour party, with its roots in trade unionism belongs to a large extent to the unions. It is in the interests of the unions to fight to get it into power. And once it is there, the unions will, as far as they possibly can, support it. The unions will want to keep it there and in identifying with its problems they are forced to identify with the economy of the country, the international banking community and all the other interests on whom the government of this country rests. Unavoidably, the union leaders lose touch with their original aims, and they are caught up in politics and inextricably bound up with the Labour party, which was in the first place only the political arm of the unions. Meanwhile, back on the factory floor, life continues as usual. The government is still the government, and the same needs, demands, grievances have still to be aired. The union executives, concerned with the strength of the Labour party, are anxious to stop strikes that rock the government The Labour party, when in opposition, is ambivalent about strikes (although strikes cause damage to the Labour party image). But when in power it was confronted by them and forced to try and stop them. As a result, the only way the same demands and grievances could be aired was unofficially.

The man I was talking to impressed me more than anyone I had met at Lucas. He talked a great deal about a number of subjects, and was extremely well-informed. He was interested in foreign policy and also talked one day at great length about how scandalous it was that the Americans included in the figures they gave for foreign aid, all the foreign investment made by private companies. He did not consider himself particularly left-wing, and had been a Labour party member all his life. He made me realize yet again how many people work at jobs far below their mental capacity. Here was an extremely intelligent and clever man who had worked in the factory for twenty years. There are so many jobs in the country that require little or no intelligence, that it cannot be true that most of the people who do them are fit for nothing else. Most people have very little chance indeed of getting away. Even if they are clever, they have to be extremely lucky to get any real opportunity to get out into something that would fulfil their potential. Even if now with comprehensive education a few more of the clever working class children do get to university, the same jobs are still there to be done, and everyone can't get out. There are still more jobs for stupid people than there could ever be stupid people to fill them.

Another interesting point about status: I asked someone one day about the man I met in the canteen. I asked if he was a shop-steward, as he seemed so politically aware. She looked surprised and said, 'Oh no, he's only a charge hand.' An elected union official ranks higher in people's minds than the firm's selected overseer.

What this man said about strikes made me understand far more than I had done.

In 1968 there were 2,350 strikes, about nine every day. That sounds like a very high figure, but given that there are 213,000 workplaces which come under the Factories Act, 376 coal mines and 103,725 farms and railway stations employing labour, while nine strikes happen, 316,991 don't, which seems to me more surprising.

Over the last five years an average of three million days has been lost because of strikes. But then, 146 million days were lost because of industrial accidents and diseases. Perhaps in the long run more legislation for safety at work would pay better dividends than legislation against strikes.

On the third day, there was a strike meeting, and almost all the strikers voted to return to work. Although it had been expected by many, including the strikers, to last for a long time, it came to an end. The reasons were complicated, but the most important one was the pressure put on them by the number of workers in the industry that were laid off. As there were only 600 strikers, they would have had to be very tough to take the responsibility for so much suffering. The other reason was that the foremen felt that their interests were not best served by combining their demands with their inferiors', the charge hands. They decided they wanted to put their claim separately, and so they voted to go back to work. Also, a number of union officials, who hate unofficial strikes more than anyone, as they undermine the unions, converged on the strikers and put every pressure on them that they could muster. But mostly it was the moral pressure of the workers who were laid off. Had the strikers not been supervisors, they could have resisted it better, but being extra-sensitive to what people thought about them, they could not easily withstand the hatred and fury levelled at them by the workers. In the factory by then there was little sympathy for them. Again, the workers would have stood by them against the management, but amongst each other, and to the strikers, they said it was wrong that a privileged group should cause harm to a lesser one.

When Bill came back to work on Thursday, there was an odd situation. Everyone avoided talking to him for having supported a strike that jeopardized their livelihoods and was of no benefit to them. But they also continued to cold-shoulder, more fiercely if anything, Norman and Mr Taylor, for having been 'black-legs' – for having stayed in while their colleagues struck.

The strike brought home to almost everyone in the shop how very insecure their apparent affluence was. Very few of them had much money saved up and they only saved for specific things, such as holidays, cars, and furniture. Overnight their income could drop by half. Those on part-time would not be able to sign on at the Labour exchange. Very few of them owned their own houses, and the lucky ones who did were mortgaged up to their ears. Although they were far better off than most workers in England, and better-paid than some white collar workers, their affluence was frighteningly superficial. The poor are very good at seeming rich as soon as they get some money. They fill their houses with washing machines, fitted carpets, gadgets of all sorts; they have cars and radios. It is a natural celebration at momentarily being released from poverty. Middle-class people living on fixed incomes, have sometimes said to me, 'But the workers are so much richer than we are. We haven't got forty pounds a week to spend.' But if they had the choice between the security of invested money that would last and appreciate till the end of their days, or comparative affluence for their working lives, permanently threatened, with the certainty that they would end up with little more than the old age pension, I have no doubt which they would choose. 'But they're so feckless,' say others. 'Why don't they save?' The answer is that they have all seen what happened to their parents' savings, how after a lifetime of pinching and scraping, the money they put by was in the end worth nothing like the sacrifices they had made to save it. They know they aren't going to better their position in any major way, so why not enjoy the money while they've got it?

Birmingham itself perfectly epitomizes this kind of superficial affluence. It is a city built for cars – three motorways converge in the centre, and the pedestrian spends most of his time in concrete subterranean passageways. The whole city centre is a grim new sea of prefabrication, with the new Bull Ring Shopping Centre as the focal point of hideousness, surrounded by criss-crossing bypasses and new roads. There is almost nothing that is old, and nothing that is new is well-designed. The city is full of new night clubs, new restaurants, smart discotheques and gambling clubs. The whole place is designed for spending money, as much as one possibly can. Everything is constantly being re-painted, re-varnished, re-fronted. Even outside the centre, on the way to work, the bus passed a small roadside cafe where 'Alf's Café' had just been painted out, and a new sign put up saying 'Alfred Wragg's Coffee House'. But Birmingham has a very serious housing problem. There are appalling slums, terrible overcrowding, and a very long waiting list for houses. The word Brummagem, originally local slang for Birmingham, means according to the Oxford Dictionary 'counterfeit, cheap, sham, showy'.

The personnel manager of the factory who took me round the whole place on my last day at Lucas's was intelligent and sympathetic, had been to university, and had worked in factories. I asked about the strike, why it happened and why it had ended. I asked why it was that 19,000 workers on car assembly lines in other factories had been laid off after only a day's strike at Lucas's. 'There is very little stock-piling in the car industry', was the answer. 'We only keep about a week's supply in store. Stock-piling is just a waste of money.'

But if there were a week's supply, why were they laid off?

It isn't unknown for the management of different firms to get together to try to get the strikers to go back to work by laying off their workers, and it seemed to me that this was something that could have happened here.

We went into the machine shop. There were enormous machines, oozing grease, filling the whole room. It looked a bit like the engine room of a big ship, and the noise was louder than almost anything I have ever heard. There were a great many people working there a far higher proportion of them coloured than anywhere else. 'That's because we have a quicker turnover of labour in this department and they've come here more recently,' the personnel manager said. I couldn't hear a word that was spoken while we were in there. 'You get used to it. I hardly notice it now.' The men working in that shop were covered in oil. 'Statistically it's very small, but there is some risk of dermatitis here.' Dermatitis can lead to scrotal cancer. 'But we provide excellent showers and washing facilities. The trouble is they put their greasy hands into the pockets of their overalls, and the oil is a special hard engine oil. But if they're clean, and they change their overalls once a week, they are quite safe. They all have medical check-ups every six months.'

As we came to one shop, full of men and women working at repairing second-hand car parts, we stopped. 'I don't think we'll go in there today. There's a bit of trouble, after the strike.' We skirted round into another shop. The trouble was that when the workers there were laid off on Monday, they were told that there would be an announcement in the local paper telling them when they should return. As it happened, the news that the strike was over came too late in the evening on Wednesday for the firm to be able to put the announcement in the paper. But some of the workers heard the news that the strike was over and they came back to work on Thursday without having been told to. On Thursday morning, confronted with about half the work force, it was decided to let them start work, as they were there, and it seemed pointless to send them home when there was work for them to do. Then the announcement was inserted and on Friday all the others came back too. But when they found that some of the workers, by pure luck, had been allowed to work the previous day, they were indignant. 'They said it wasn't fair, and that those who turned up on Thursday should have been sent home,' I was told. But the unions were called in and there was trouble about it. The personnel manager was in a difficult position having tried to do what seemed best. It was thought there would have been more trouble if they had been sent home on Thursday. All strikes, and union problems, were dealt with by the personnel manager.

The management knew that I was at the factory to write about it. I had arranged it all beforehand, as it was not the sort of place that you could wander into and get a job straight away. There was very little coming and going amongst the workers there. For that reason my presence was thought a little strange by the other women, but they accepted my explanation that I was a student doing holiday work. The foremen and charge hands were not told either but they may have suspected that I was there to do some sort of research.

All the women were overwhelmingly friendly and as I was young, curiously protective. When they heard I was living in digs with a Polish family in one of the worst parts of Birmingham, they were anxious about me, and Carla would bring extra sandwiches for me at lunchtime. Carla made me promise that I would write to her when I got home and I said I would, but when I sat down to write I found that I couldn't.

Although she knew I was a student at Oxford, she entirely failed to grasp the fact that my life was and always would be quite different to hers. Her knowledge of a middle class life was only visualized through a cloud of smoke, as being like her own life if she had more money. In describing my life to her I was, I suppose, anxious not to rub in the differences, but without actually lying I could see my words as they passed from my lips and entered her ears being translated instantly from one class to another. Her frame of reference was necessarily narrow. She could only imagine what she knew, and she was more or less unaware of the privileges she didn't have.

While I was there, working in the factory, and living in digs, it was easy to believe my own account of myself and to make friends. But when I got back to my own life, I couldn't write to Carla and tell her I had lied, and had been talking to her only so as to write about her. I couldn't tell her that I had only been working there so as to write about it, that I hadn't needed to work there at all, that I had only been doing out of interest what she was forced to do for the whole of her life.

Chapter Five

# Army

'This could be you,' reads a poster outside the central London recruiting office. There is a picture of a pretty girl smiling in a green uniform.

There was no one waiting in the waiting-room, with its bleak, shiny green and cream paint. In the corner there was a big photograph of the corps pop group: five women in uniform, a mascot poodle and a drum-kit with 'The Militaires' written across it.

The recruiting captain in her office was looking through my papers on the desk in front of her. 'Of course I'm no psychologist,' she said, 'but it seems to me that you've had an insecure childhood, and the army can offer you the security you need.' After three intelligence tests and two interviews, it was suggested that I was best suited to the military police.

I signed on for six years, with an option – which applies to the whole army – of getting out at six weeks. The captain handed me a small black soldiers' bible, already inscribed with my name. I took it in my right hand and swore to be loyal to the Queen, her heirs and successors, and I was given a free travel pass down to Guildford for the following Monday morning.

The Queen Elizabeth barracks in Guildford is the training depot for the Women's Royal Army Corps. Coming into the camp through the gates guarded by regimental policewomen, the first thing one sees is the huge tarmac parade ground that dominates the whole barracks. Otherwise the place looks like one of the grimmer new universities. As I stood there looking round, I could hear singing. Suddenly round the corner came a platoon of girls, marching along with their arms swinging, feet stamping, and belting out at the tops of their voices, 'Inky Pinky Parlez-vous'.

When I found my room, there were four beds in it. One girl was already there, sitting on a chair with her suitcase at her feet. She looked at me carefully and then said, 'I'm Janice. The others haven't arrived yet.' She added emphatically, 'I hope they're the sort of girls who'll pull their weight.' She was a large, bland fair girl who was hoping to go into the military police. 'My father was in the police force,' she said. Her brother was in the army and she admired him more than anyone in the world. She told me, within five minutes of meeting, that she had taken O levels, been head girl of her school for two years running, and had always wanted to join the army.

The other two girls in my room arrived later. Jacqueline, from Norfolk, hoped to be a physical training instructor, and was already a high jump champion. She was seventeen, small, and gentle. She had a teddy bear which she often talked to for comfort. Janice, the military policewoman, took to looking after Jacqueline like a mother.

The fourth girl was Dawn. Tall and clumsy, she talked without drawing breath, mentioning friends and relations as if we knew them as well as she did. She was an orphan who had been brought up by her two older sisters, and she talked in her sleep at night and cried because she missed her boyfriend. Whenever we were given orders, Dawn asked endless questions which infuriated the rest of the platoon, but she was the only one who was indignant at the way we were treated.

Reveille was at six thirty; breakfast at seven fifteen; and at eight fifteen was stand-by-bed inspection, when every floor, corridor and stair had to be immaculate, without dust or marks. Our uniform had to be properly washed and ironed, and our big black beetle-crushers had to shine like patent leather. The corporal yelled down the corridor, 'Stand by your beds!' We stood in silence for half an hour until she yelled, 'Room 'shun!' and the officer inspected us. Our room was at the end of the passage, and the dust settled in the half hour it took her to reach us. We usually had to clean the whole room again.

After inspection the corporal bellowed out, 'Six platoon! Outside in squad! Last one out gets extra duties!' Thirty-two of us scrambled out of the block to a strip of tarmac, grabbing our berets. 'If she gives me extra duties, I'll bloody smash her face in,' said Irma from the room next door, but we ran all the same. We were marched out on to the parade ground for drill.

It was a blistering hot day. The corporal demonstrated drill as we stood at ease, a small breeze blowing at our long green skirts and sweaty green Aertex shirts. 'Squad! Left turn, in threes, right turn!' We did our best. 'Which way does she bloody mean?' Pat whispered and found herself facing the rest of the squad.

'Private Johnson, you're thick! What are you?'

'I'm thick, Sergeant,' she answered quickly. We were marched away again to the education centre for lectures.

From then on, everywhere we went, we were marched.

The course of lectures was opened by the Commandant of the barracks herself. She was a tall and gracious woman in her late forties, well-preserved, with neatly curled short fair hair, tucked under her forage cap. She spoke like the Duchess of Kent, who is second in charge of the Corps.

She gave rather a surprising talk. 'You may have heard that the British army is pulling out of many of the countries where we are stationed, and I know that most of you are looking forward to foreign postings. But I think you will find that whenever the British army is pulling out of one country, we are going into another.' She then listed all the countries where the W.R.A.C. is posted – including, oddly enough, Cambodia and Vietnam.

The young second lieutenants, fresh from officer training school, were pretty and anxious to please, and seemed rather insecure about their position. One young platoon officer lectured us on 'Ranks and Badges'. 'When an officer or an N.C.O. tells you to jump out of the window, you jump,' she said. 'If you wish to do so you may question the command, after you have obeyed it.' Someone asked if officers went through the ranks. 'No,' she said. 'There isn't time.' She looked round the room a little nervously. 'Mind you,' she added, 'I think you're awfully lucky to be in the ranks. If I could start again, I'd go into the ranks. There's so much more variety, and you've no idea how boring it is sometimes in the officers' mess, with nothing but all those old women to talk to.' Her audience didn't look particularly convinced.

The hierarchy in the W.R.A.C. is absolutely rigid; the privates are so untouchable that even the lance-corporals have different lavatories and bathrooms. The officers live quite separately. They have to be saluted and called Ma'am. Several times I found myself turning and walking in the opposite direction if I saw someone coming who might have been an officer, so that I wouldn't have to decide whether to salute. The first officer I saluted made me do it again three times for sloppiness.

The officers' training lasts eight months, and the brochures say that it is usual for officers to have two A levels. I got the impression that this wasn't the only qualification; many of them came from army families and they all had middle-class voices. The officers are kept quite apart from the ranks. If they fail to pass through their training, they have to leave the army altogether – they cannot be demoted to the ranks. We weren't allowed within two hundred yards of their quarters.

One officer gave us a lecture on hygiene. The captain's opening lines were, 'I always say that you can lead a W.R.A.C. girl to the bath, but you can't wash her.' Then she told us about VD. 'Of course, if you only associate with the sort of boys your parents would like you to associate with, there is no danger at all.' Thus she perpetuated a dangerous myth.

The girls were impressed by the lectures. 'They're kind, aren't they?' said a girl sitting next to me. The officers could afford the luxury of trying to please, in a rather patronising, condescending way, while the N.C.O.s only had time for bossing and bullying. 'The difference' said a second lieutenant, 'between an officer and an N.C.O. is the difference between a prefect and a teacher.'

A red-haired Captain lectured us on Responsibilities, Rights and Privileges. In our notebooks we copied down three columns from the blackboard:

Responsibilities – 1. Loyalty (to Queen and Army); 2. Pride in personal turnout and property; 3. Discipline (to obey orders).

Rights – 1. Medical and dental care; 2. Right to draw pay; 3. Right to food or ration allowance; 4. Right to discharge during first six weeks or after three months on payment of fifteen pounds.

Privileges – 1. Leave (no basic right to leave); 2. Social amenities (Naafi, library, ping-pong, etc.); 3. Legal aid for defence at a court martial; 4. The wearing of civvies when not on duty.

Someone did point out that by any trade union standard the privileges would be rights, but she only muttered and the officer didn't hear. That was Angela, who had decided to leave after three days.

At the end of the third week, halfway through basic training, we were to have an exam. We would be tested on everything about the W.R.A.C. and the army, including the corps motto – Gentle in manner, resolute in deed – a brief history of the corps, and the names of all the officers in the camp.

To help us with the exam, one afternoon we were taken round the W.R.A.C. museum. On show were the chassis of the car the Queen learned to drive in during the war, the dress the Queen Mother wore in the officers' mess in 1955, a drum or two, a broken biscuit left over from the first World War, a few photographs, and a miniature silver gun. W.R.A.C. tea towels were on sale at 37½p each.

With some amazement, most of the recruits accepted all this. 'It's like beginning all over again,' Connie said in the washroom. 'Like when you first go to school.' She was a fat complacent girl from Leeds. Her mother was a cripple. She had had twelve jobs since leaving school two years ago, and her mother thought it was about time she 'did something with her life'. She was miserably homesick but didn't dare leave, she explained, because of what her mother would say'.

For the recruits, minute regulations govern every minute of the day. All day long the N.C.O.s are watching – shouting about stray hairs escaping from under berets, yelling about scuff marks on shoes or the foot that isn't in step in the squad. If we had a few minutes to spare, feet aching from marching for hours in hard shoes, we couldn't sit on our bed because a bed with a small bump in it might be stripped at any time in the day. We couldn't smoke, either, because we weren't allowed to use the ashtrays during the day. We sat on hard chairs, trying to keep our black shoes – saturated with polish – from making marks on the very receptive pale lino floor.

The recruits who were staying were passive and were kept too busy to think. The ones who were leaving hated it, but weren't indignant. Women without men are rarely political animals and they don't often shout for their rights. They either stayed or left, but didn't complain.

On Wednesdays we got paid. We had to queue for half an hour, salute and say Ma'am in order to get the pay to which we were entitled. The pay for recruits is £2.51 per day. We were told in the brochures that this was good money as everything else is found, but that wasn't quite true. For instance, the last meal in the day is at four thirty, so by the time we had finished work at seven thirty or later, everyone needed to buy a meal in the Naafi, which was not particularly cheap. Also, although everything had to be kept spotlessly clean, hardly any of the things we needed to keep the rooms up to inspection standards were provided. So much of our income was spent on soap powder, dusters, shoe polish, furniture polish, Windolene, nametapes, shoe trees, starch, etc.

The pay doesn't rise very much later. In a complicated pay scheme, the average lance-corporal receives £3.74 per day, a corporal £4.33 per day, and a sergeant £4.92 per day. The officers get a bit more – £1573 a year for a second lieutenant, about £1887 for a lieutenant. A lieutenant-colonel gets £4497 after twenty-five years' service.

Why were they prepared to put up with it? Out of my 'intake' of one hundred and thirty girls, forty decided to leave – ten from each platoon. Pat, a short and violent red-head from Scotland said, 'If you came from where I come from, it'd seem like a holiday camp. It's a good life and you have to work hard wherever you are. In my time off I'm freer than I ever was. No parents breathing down my neck. Plenty of fellas and no fussing.' She was a capable girl, determined and obedient, and she bullied the girls who complained. 'What are you? Soft or something?' she'd shout at the ones who grumbled about the N.C.O.s.

Eva was in the same room as Pat. When they were together they victimized the weak and miserable girls who wanted to go home. 'What did you join the fucking army for? You didn't think it was a bed of bleeding roses, did you?' I heard her shout at Elsie.

Elsie came from London. Within a few hours of arriving she had said she wanted to leave. She came from a family of fourteen and said that she had been pushed out of home, aged fifteen, because there wasn't room. She talked about herself obsessively and told a great many stories, some of which were hard to believe. She said she had self-induced abortions every three months. She spent all her pay the day she got it and was untidy, not very clean, and persecuted.

Next to me in the front of the squad was Milly. We developed a technique of whispering to one another without the N.C.O.s noticing. She was a lumpish dark girl with a severe twitch and constant cold sores on her lip. Her mother had bullied her into joining up, and wouldn't let her leave although she was miserable. Her mother had married again and didn't want her at home. Before you can leave the army, you have to have permission from a parent – and her mother wouldn't give it. At first Milly seemed quite wretched and downtrodden, but she had a fund of rage that overflowed sometimes, in spite of her stammer.

Another girl, Marlene, told me, 'I joined because I wanted to get married.' She grinned and added, 'It worked.' Her boyfriend wrote to her within three days of her arrival at the barracks, proposing marriage, and she accepted at once. For her it was a bit like joining the Foreign Legion.

But in this 'intake' there was a much higher proportion of girls who wanted to leave than was usual. The officers were worried. I heard that the Commandant had held a special meeting with the training N.C.O.s to try to find out what was going wrong.

At the end of our first week was the Passing Out parade of the intake ahead of us. It was another hot day and we started the morning by putting out chairs. We were lined up to watch on one side. Friends and relations of the passing out recruits were on the other side, some with cine cameras, many with proud parental smiles.

The band appeared in the distance: euphoniums, cornets, clarinets, trumpets, xylophones, drums, trombones and tubas, bright and glittering in the sun. They were playing, the programme said, 'Hey, Look Me Over' as they came striding out on to the parade ground. The drum major was dressed from head to foot in a leopard skin, and the band's uniforms were shiny with buckles and buttons. They played the company on, and platoon by platoon the girls came stamping out, perfectly in time, arms swinging waist high, chins and chests out, heads held high. A colonel, resplendent with medals, took the salute, and we stood for the regimental march, 'The Lass of Richmond Hill'. Officers like Royalty inspected the troops to 'Greensleeves', and the girls and the band marched away.

The rest of the morning we put the chairs away again. We were all moved by the band music, and most of the recruits were feeling cheered and exhilarated. Some of them were singing a song they had picked up from the passing out company:

It wasn't the Wrens who won the war,
The girls in green were there before.
It wasn't the Wrens who got the Yanks,
The girls in green were there in tanks.
It wasn't the Wrens who were first in bed,
The girls in green were way ahead.
Inky pinky parlez-vous.

As they stacked up the chairs, others were singing, 'Pack up your troubles in your old kit bag and smile, smile, smile.'

The new recruits seemed on the whole gentle, innocent and childish, but the girls who had been there for some time were a rough, tough, hard drinking and hard swearing lot. They came to blows sometimes and there were nasty stories about a girl who found razor blades in her pillow one night. I saw a fight one evening between two girls who were punching each other like boxers.

From the day we arrived we were given strict instructions to have nothing to do with either of the other two companies stationed there. It wasn't explained why. 'It's for your own good, like all the rules,' the Sergeant said.

None of the recruits seemed to be lesbians, but there were quite a few among those who had been there longer. I thought that almost all the training N.C.O.s were. They had volunteered to come back to this barracks, all female, to train the recruits. One evening at dusk a whole platoon of girls leaned out of their windows and watched one girl kissing another. One of the girls was a Corporal – she yelled at them 'Get back in those windows!' They were shocked by the experience, although they laughed.

While I was there the Commandant banned trousers in the evenings because she said too many of the girls were taking advantage of the privilege in order to make themselves appear masculine. It was generally accepted that recruits were left alone for the first six weeks, but after that they were fair game. On the train coming back, a girl told me that lesbians wore black signet rings on their fingers and gold rings on their little fingers to identify themselves. I have no idea how widespread it was, and probably it was talked and gossiped about more than it actually happened.

On my first weekend we were allowed out for the first time. On Saturday night Eva, Dawn, Irma and I went down to the discotheque in Guildford. The town was packed with soldiers. That part of the country around Aldershot is bursting with barracks. We walked the two miles to the town centre to save the bus fare. Some young boys began following us, shouting 'Wracs, Wracs, Wracs!' Dawn told me, 'You know what that stands for? Weekly Ration of Army Cunt.'

The discotheque was hot and murky. We met up with some soldiers from Aldershot who had two bottles of whisky, which they mixed with beer and red wine. We all got very drunk. Dawn, who was five foot ten, was picked up by a tiny Welsh soldier who kept saying, 'You like me, don't you? You want to go with me, don't you?' She kept saying no. Eventually Eva shouted at him across the room, 'You! Leave my recruit alone! I'm her Sergeant and I won't have you touching up my recruits!' and he slunk away.

I met a Yorkshire man who talked a good deal about the Reds, and the Blacks, and the Yellow Peril. He made Irma and me have a competition to see if we could drink a bottle of beer quicker than he and the Welshman could drink two. We were sick in the street outside. 'What's the women's army for anyhow?' said the Yorkshire man. 'Just a load of mattresses for the men.'

Back in the camp, girls were sick all night. Some of them had never had a drink before in their lives. For those under eighteen, drunkenness was a seriously punishable offence. For the others, a blind eye was turned by the N.C.O.s as long as they were sober enough to remember their numbers as they came through the gate.

Several of us sat up talking quite late. 'I met a fella with a mini-van with a bed in the back,' Pat said. 'What do they think we are?' On the whole, the recruits were respectable girls who kept clear of sex, had boyfriends at home who wrote them letters, and had until then led well-protected lives with angry fathers who checked on all their movements. Many of them seemed rather bewildered by the strictness of the rules within the camp, and the total unprotected freedom they were allowed outside it.

On Sunday night, Elsie and I went over to the men's barracks at Aldershot, where we'd been invited by the soldiers we met the night before. Elsie said she thought she was pregnant again and said, 'Going with a bloke helps get rid of it,' and she disappeared with two soldiers almost as soon as we got there. But she was an exception and the other girls were shocked by her behaviour. I sat in the Naafi where the soldiers were singing obscene songs and the beer was swilling around on the floor. 'The army's no place for a woman,' said the Yorkshireman I had met in the discotheque. 'I'd never marry a W.R.A.C., I can tell you.'

The weekend depressed most of the girls. They felt they should have had a good time, but somehow most of them hadn't.

Most of the girls had joined up in a surprisingly casual way; they had seen advertisements in magazines and filled out the forms, or caught sight of a poster in the labour exchange, or wandered into a glittering new recruiting office out of curiosity. Many of them hadn't thought much about it before, and finding themselves suddenly away from home for the first time, in a totally strange and alien world were appalled and terrified by it.

The ones who had led a particularly protected life seemed to feel that this was what life outside the family was. Although it seemed strange to them, many of them assumed that there was nothing so very odd about the army as a way of life, and they tried very hard to accept it.

Many of them for one reason or another had had such unhappy lives that they didn't any longer think in terms of whether or not they were happy. A very high proportion of them came from seriously disrupted backgrounds. They didn't make it as easy for themselves as they might have done, by sticking together, by encouraging a sense of solidarity. I suspect that women are much worse at living together in a community than men. The code of loyalty to each other and solidarity in the men's army that helps make life liveable doesn't really exist among women. It was not particularly frowned upon for girls to tell on one another to the N.C.O.s, and the N.C.O.s didn't hesitate to report people to the officers.

At times the N.C.O.s did make rough attempts at popularity with the platoon. When they made jokes we laughed our heads off. 'Cheer up! We haven't made you sweep the floors with your eyelashes yet!' joked the Sergeant.

Since leaving the army I have worked at other jobs, in factories and offices, and I think I have come to look on it with more sympathy. I understand a little better what makes girls join up. The girls who joined seemed to me to be slightly above average intelligence and to be more adventurous than others. Most of them had the added incentive of an unhappy home life, but one of the most important factors was that they had all had jobs which they hadn't liked. Ahead of them had been the prospect of a whole life spent in the same town, with the same people, doing the same job until – and perhaps after – they got married. While I was in the army I thought it so dreadful that anything would have been better. The way we were shouted at all day, the way we were treated as barely human, the absurdity of the jobs we spent most of the day doing, the total lack of privacy and control over one's life – these things oppressed me more than anything. And yet I am not at all sure that if I lived somewhere like Birmingham and did a job as unpleasant and cripplingly boring as the one I did at the Cake factory, that I wouldn't much rather get out and away, find a different life, get abroad for a couple of years, meet new people and so on, in spite of the nastiness of most aspects of army life.

I can see why most of them joined, and I could see what they were getting away from, but I cannot understand why it is that life in the women's army has to be made so unpleasant. It would be very easy for women to do all the same jobs in the army without any of the military trappings, the rules, the discipline or the marching.

The women's army, we were told over and over again in our lectures, exists in order to take over a great many administrative and non-combative jobs from men who could then be released to do the fighting at the front. We were all going to be trained as typists, cooks, chauffeurs, truck drivers, potato peelers, bat women, telephone operators and – a very few of us – semi-skilled radio operators and intelligence clerks: jobs not so very different in themselves to jobs outside the army. As I have always understood it, military discipline and learning to obey every order – however absurd – without question, is designed to teach men to obey the most absurd order of them all, to go out and get themselves killed. But women never fight, never handle guns and would never get nearer a battle than the typing pool at headquarters. The women's army is modelled exactly on the men's, and it seemed like retarded tomboys playing at soldiers for the fun of it – only somewhere along the line they had managed to get the indulgence of the Ministry of Defence. It would have been easy to devise a system where women worked for the men's army in the same way that they would have done any other job, and they would have had a much better time. Nearly all that bullying and bossing could be done away with tomorrow.

In my platoon of thirty-two, eleven of us wanted to leave. We went to see the sergeant at the end of the first week. She said our resignations wouldn't be considered until the end of the second week. They could have kept us for all six weeks of the basic training, and I suspect that only those who went on and on complaining were allowed out before then.

At the end of our second week we had an English exam, in which we had to answer three questions. First, we had to write a comprehension piece on an extract from *'Doctor at Large'*, then an essay on 'Woman's place is in the home', and finally, 'Imagine you are writing an article for *Lioness* (the corps magazine), describing your first week in the army'. By this time I was desperate to get out, and I wrote ten pages of vitriolic attack and the next day I was summoned to the Company Commander, who was sitting in her office with my essay on her desk.

I came into the room and – as I was instructed – saluted and announced, 'Private Toynbee, Ma'am.' She began by being severe, but turned out to be the only reasonable person I had talked to. She agreed with some of what I had written and began to explain why she was there. 'I look on the army almost as a social service,' she said. 'So many girls need the security. I enjoy helping them and I feel that for a lot of them we can broaden their horizons and give them a chance to have experiences they would never have in any other way.' To her the army was a final safety net for people who have slipped through school, youth employment officers, social workers, or anyone else who might have helped them before, at the age of seventeen, the army became the only answer. I agreed with her, but pointed out that first, there was something wrong with a society that made the wretched life in the army preferable to anything else. Secondly, even if some girls did need the army to lean on, that was no reason to treat them so inhumanly. Few of them were there because it was so unpleasant, but in spite of it. Her attitude was like the Victorian view of how work houses should be. Nonetheless, she was a sympathetic woman who would have liked to make changes.

I don't think that she or anyone else guessed what I was doing there. I was surprised that the girls didn't think me as odd as they might have done. The N.C.O.s wouldn't have noticed anything different about me because to them there was no possibility that anyone could be different from anyone else. Until that day I had never spoken to an officer. The Company Commander was worried by the number of recruits leaving on this intake, and she accused me of stirring up discontent. 'Always happens when you have officer material in the ranks,' she said, to my surprise. (All I had done was to write an explicit essay. Apart from my rather noticeable but unavoidable incompetence, I had remained anonymous.) She said I would be discharged as soon as possible, the next morning.

In my last day I went through everything I had done at first in reverse order. I took back my kit, was signed off at the education centre, had another blanket check and got signatures on my discharge form from various officers. I was kept well away from the others, and everything was rushed through with what seemed suddenly like indecent haste. I had another medical and was told that in two weeks I had lost five pounds and grown half an inch. I had to refund the underclothes allowance they had given me of £8.37½p, and also a day's pay of 84p. Then I was taken to see the Commandant herself.

After my last interview I expected her to be reasonable too. I had made a miscalculation. 'Private Toynbee, why do you think people join the army?' she asked coldly. I gave her what I thought to be a reasonable but polite answer. 'Because for some people who are emotionally insecure, it offers things they have missed.'

'The army, Private Toynbee, is not a place for underprivileged inadequates!' she answered sharply. 'It offers a chance to serve, which you will never get again. It is a splendid opportunity for any girl, one which you have chosen to reject.' I saluted and left.

I was told I was to take all my belongings with me when I went to collect my final demob papers. As I walked away from the documents office, carying my kit bag, my suitcase and my papers, my platoon came by, marching smartly in squad, out on to the hot parade ground. As they went marching past, one girl whispered to me, 'Kiss all the fellas for me in civvy street.'

Chapter Six

# Soap

Most overpowering of all was the smell. There was soap everywhere, within a mile's radius there was enough soap in the air to make your nose itch all the time. Sometimes it smelt like Lifebuoy, sometimes like Surf, and sometimes the smell was sulphurous and chemical. Then there was the constant roar from the factories. The main gate was at one end of the village, and at night the factory glowed in the dark and the roaring was louder, like an aeroplane constantly circling overhead. With soap everywhere one wouldn't have been surprised if the air itself had burst into bubbles when it rained. In fact, sometimes when there was rain after a long dry spell, foam did appear on the roofs and in the gutters.

It was dark early on a Sunday evening when I arrived in Port Sunlight. I came by bus from Birkenhead and through the rain and dark I stared out at the characterless gloom of the houses, strung together along the grim side of the Mersey. There is nothing to be said for Birkenhead. It grew up at the beginning of the century around a few factories, with no centre, no beginning and no end; street after street of bleak and dreadful houses, with none of the photogenic starkness of Northern towns. Across the Mersey from Liverpool, these areas stretch out their grimy tentacles in all directions.

Port Sunlight village is outside Birkenhead in Bebington, another shambling and depressed town.

I got off the bus and walked into the village. It was dimly lit by horrible yellow sodium lights, and suddenly I was in another world. After the streets of Birkenhead and Bebington I was in a place like Disneyland. The little mock Tudor houses with strips of green grass in front of them looked like cardboard chalets. There were curious monuments looming up out of the yellow-lit dark, hideous and magnificent. Lines of small trees, a Roman Temple, an Italian garden, Gothic halls, an odd little church; everything was tiny. The place was so clean and orderly, to the last regulation blade of grass that you felt you had been swept into a model village in Harrods toy department and that you were rather too large for the buildings and the trees. And all of this was the grand insane fantasy of one man, Lord Leverhulme.

Although it was only nine o'clock, there was no one to be seen in the village. The streets were deserted and it took me a long time to find my lodgings.

I began work straight away the next morning. The company arranges an induction procedure which begins with a film about the company and dangers to be avoided at work. There were a number of other new employees that week. We were told of the 'tidiest department' competition, which was held every so often – in fact not many of the workers I met had heard of it. After the film we were taken to the big new medical centre, a well-designed, light, airy building, where we were thoroughly inspected, tested and questioned and told repeatedly to report sick at the centre for the least cut, bruise or headache. Then we were shown to our jobs. I was the only new employee to be sent to the Scourers Department.

Walking down the corridors of number 3 block to the Scourers Department you have to pass along a balcony overhanging the Lux soapery. In there everything is white. The dust, the floor, the air. You can smell it coming yards away down the passage. You begin to sneeze. Your nose itches unbearably the closer you get to the soap. From that moment on I would sneeze for twenty minutes on end, every day. As you walked along the balcony, the smell of soap and scent is quite extraordinarily strong. I think I should have been sick very often if I had had to work in that department.

In the Scourers Department Vim was being made, and also a lavatory cleaner called Dot. The main entrance to the department is from the balcony that runs along from the Lux soapery, with wooden stairs leading down to the shopfloor.

I had come to expect to be confused on walking into a factory for the first time. However grim the work is and however wretched the conditions, the beauty of the machines is startling. I am excited by the noise and the speed at which everything happens. The colours and sounds merge into one vibrating blur, each component perfectly synchronized. Everything in the room contrasted oddly with the glittering bright product, the packets of Vim, familiar but looking strange as so many of them poured off the line together.

One corner of the room was partitioned off by barriers and there were two rows of formica topped tables and three vending machines for hot and cold drinks and Mars bars, for tea breaks.

This room was concerned only with the packing of Vim and Dot. The powder came cascading from the floors above down pipes at one end of the packing line. When I asked them, no one seemed to know where the powder came from. They shrugged and said it came from the pipes, unaware of the people upstairs who were actually making it. As far as they were concerned where it came from and what it was made of didn't matter. They only saw it as it came along the belt in open canisters.

The powder is a bright blue-green and the room was covered in a faint blue haze. The dust that lay on the walls, the machines, the floors, was all bluish grey, and it gets in your hair, and eyes and clothes and under your finger-nails. The other women said it took three months to get used to it, and to stop sneezing.

Vim is sold in various shapes and sizes. I was working on a fancy pack, a small pink and blue canister with a plastic embossed pattern on it. It was a masterpiece of hideousness, a genteel and horrid little canister called a 'Bathroom Pack'.

Five of us worked at the machine turning these out. For most of the time I was sitting down at the conveyor belt, watching the canisters go by as they came out of the machine that put the lids on. I had to take out the ones with faulty lids. At the next stage along the line the canisters were turned on their sides, so if I missed a lidless one, all the Vim would spill out and pour on to the floor or into the machinery.

About twice an hour, the machine that put the lids on would get stuck and every canister that went by would have to be taken out. They went by at a great pace and it was difficult to get every single one of them off the line. You leapt to your feet and pulled them off the belt in handfuls, but there was nowhere to put them. You had to stack them on the floor around you, balance them on the machine until you found yourself standing in a sea of canisters. Then, when the machine was working again, you would feed them back on to the line, putting tops on them by hand, squeezing them in with the new lot coming along the belt, so that even if the machine went wrong several times a day, the same number of canisters was still turned out. Just as you reached the end of your stockpile, the machine would break down and you had to start stacking again. It wasn't really hard work, but it dragged.

An unofficial, but universally recognized system operated in the department called 'spelling'. The management had always accepted and catered for it, while pretending to turn a blind eye. On our machine there were five of us to do the work of four people. On the whole floor there was probably one more or less spare person for every ten. The spare person would come up to you and say 'Shall I spell you?' and take your place while you went to the lavatory for a smoke and a talk. A 'spell' could last for five or six minutes, and when you came back you would 'spell' someone else. If you stayed out longer the supervisor came to look for you. On average I got a 'spell' an hour which was more than people on other machines. Although we hid it from the supervisor, our machine was ridiculously overmanned.

But a lot of the pleasure went out of the 'spells' in the second week I was there. There was a ladies cloakroom that had been there since the factory was built in the 1880's. There were no lockers, just rows of hooks, and the lavatories had half doors so you could see who was inside. There were too, rows of old showers from the days when most people didn't have baths at home. The custodian of the cloakroom was a bleary-eyed old woman. She loved all the factory women and sat all day on a small heater by the lavatories talking rapidly to each of the women for their five minute spells. Sometimes on cold days she'd have cups of tea ready for her favourites. People gave her cigarettes and were glad to have her in there to talk to.

While I was there the cloakroom was closed down. The space was needed for a new department; a new cloakroom had been built at the other end of the department and they were going to pull the old one down. Milly was miserable. She was being retired and a new woman was to supervise the new cloakroom. She didn't want to retire and there were tears in her eyes for several days. On the last day of the old cloakroom she brought some cocktail biscuits, a bottle of sweet sherry and some tiny painted sherry glasses. She wept all day and gave everyone sherry and biscuits as we came in for a 'spell', and she promised to come back and see us often.

Then the new cloakroom was opened. It was huge and luxurious, glistening with pink tiles, new wash basins and all sorts of luxuries, except that there was nowhere to sit. The new attendant who had been with the firm a long time, but was new to the department and these women, was strict, and to everyone's horror, forbade smoking. 'It's fire regulations,' she said, and she didn't fraternize at all with the women, considering herself in some mysterious way, to be part of the management. The women decided to go back to the old cloakroom for 'spells'. They found Milly still there, looking about in bewilderment, and the place was locked. She hadn't really been able to believe that the old job wouldn't be there any more.

The women were angry, but as smoking and 'spells' had never been official they didn't have much redress. Some of them muttered about going to the union about it, but they didn't think much of the officious shop steward in the department, so it's unlikely a complaint ever got lodged. 'Spells' were an important part of the day. They mercifully broke the monotony and smokers badly need a cigarette.

From time to time all of us on the Bathroom Packs would change places, and I would do one of the other jobs. One person fed the canisters into a machine that wrapped them two at a time in Cellophane. The machine really did this itself, but it was established that a person should stand there and pretend; the Supervisor didn't realize and that was the easiest job.

The wrapped canisters came out of two shutters on to a conveyor belt and two packers had to put them into cardboard boxes at exactly the speed they were ejected from the wrapper. If they dropped one, fumbled or missed a move the canisters would pile up and tumble on to the floor. One person packed while the other made up a new cardboard box. When the first packer had filled her box, the second moved in quickly and so on until the end of the day. At first I could hardly manage the high-speed packing at all, but then it became automatic, but very tiring.

In Norway there is a mountain belonging to Lever Brothers. Vim is made up 90 per cent of rock quarried from the mountain and brought by ship to Port Sunlight dock. It is an ordinary hard white rock called felspar, which is ground up in enormous machines into a fine white dust. Two men on their own run the whole huge complex of computerized grinding machinery. The rest of the making of Vim is done by five other men. That makes seven men to make the product, and a hundred people to pack it. 'The packaging,' said an administration manager, 'is, after all, more important in an industry as competitive as ours.' The dust level in the grinding department is quite alarming although legally acceptable. I felt I could hardly breathe, just walking through it. The stone dust is then conveyed across to another building where a small amount of detergent, colouring, and a sickly perfume is added. This is all shaken up together and sent down a shute to be packed in the room where I was working. On the floors where the different ingredients are added, the dust level was higher, the sweet scented smell cloying and nauseous. It was very high indeed the day I was shown round by the manager of the Vim department because a dust extractor had gone wrong and there was much more around than usual. The manager said: 'No dust is good dust.' This dust level, however, was well below the maximum prescribed by law.

Until three years ago Vim was made with silicone. When the dust from that got in your lungs it stayed there for life, and the workers lived in terror of silicosis. When the Vim fell from the pipes straight to the floor, missing the canisters, which it did from time to time, and the dust blew up in clouds into the packing room, everyone would down tools and run for the door. To reduce the risk Vim is now made with felspar, which does eventually clear from the lungs, and no one talks much about fear of the dust.

But Dot, the lavatory cleaner made in the same department, is dangerous stuff. A great many precautions are taken with it, and the women who worked on that packing line spent a lot of time mopping the floor round the machines and the conveyor belts, to reduce the amount of dust. Our packing machine broke down very regularly and once when we had stopped work for almost an hour, we were sent to take over from the women working on Dot. It was doing more or less the same job, watching for light or heavy weight canisters, and watching for faulty tops. It was impossible not to be handling the powder all the time. I spilt some by mistake on my tights, and they came out in huge holes. The other women laughed and said it happened all the time, and they claimed new pairs of tights from the company.

There was very little full time work for women at Levers. They were trying to get everyone on to three part time shifts of five hours each, seven to twelve, twelve to five, and five to ten. The point of this was that in a five hour shift there is only one ten minute break, so that with three shifts a day the company gets fifteen working hours a day from the machines, with only half an hour in all lost for breaks. With full time workers, the company loses an hour in every nine, for dinner. Almost all the women working there were married, and most of them had children aged fourteen upwards. There were a few young mothers who worked the five to ten shift. They waited for their husbands to come home, and left their young children with them. It meant that they hardly saw their husbands at all. 'That's probably why they do it,' one manager said.

Dora, who was working on the same machine, had only been further than Liverpool once in her life. When she was sixteen she went to London for two days to stay with a friend and never saw more of it than Streatham. That was the only holiday she ever had. She was nearly fifty, lively and witty and she talked a great deal. She was a widow, with a fourteen year old daughter, and she lived in a council house in Birkenhead. In this factory I met more people who had hardly travelled at all than I met anywhere else.

Birkenhead isn't a rich town and I suppose they had a bit less money than people in other places I went to, but they did seem to be particularly insular. 'I don't quite know why I've never had a holiday,' Dora said. 'I've never saved the money. Well there's never been much to save. And then holidays come up on you so suddenly, don't they? You've no time to plan. Anyway, where would I go? Sometimes in the summer I sit in the park in Birkenhead, and the birds are singing and the grass is green and the sun is shining, and I think to myself, "Isn't it beautiful?" Now what's the point of going off somewhere else to see the same things?' If she had lived in a cardboard box she'd have said the same thing about the pinhole of light that came through a crack. I stopped worrying about whether I was judging other people's lives by my own, not necessarily superior, set of values. Birkenhead park! Another woman who'd never been on holiday said, 'Well, you can't miss what you've never had, can you?' and I think that's somewhere near the truth.

I asked Dora where she'd go if she could go anywhere she wanted in the world. She thought for a little and then said, 'Russia, I'd go to Russia.' Why? 'I just want to see for myself. The papers and everyone says it doesn't work, but I want to go and have a look. They say that even in Russia there's still a rich and a poor, but I want to make sure.' I asked if she'd ever been a communist. 'Oh no, I don't hold with communism at all. But all the same, I'd like to make sure.'

One woman I was working with was a Girl Guide mistress in her spare time. When anyone asked me what I was doing I said I was a student from Oxford doing holiday work. 'What's it like there?' she asked 'Is there much Guiding at Oxford?' She, and almost everyone else there had not the remotest conception of what university was. They knew it was important, and almost the only way to better one's way of life. Over and over again people said, 'Well of course if I'd had the opportunity, if I'd been to college, things would have been different.' But beyond this fact people tended to imagine university in any way that pleased them. For this woman it was a paradise of Girl Guides, for quite a few others it was a heaven of sex, dance-halls and grants. Most people knew of someone who knew of someone whose child had gone to college, and that could mean anything from a day release course at a technical college as part of an apprenticeship, to a domestic science diploma, to an honours degree. What sort of chances did their children have of going to university? On the face of it they probably had some sort of equality of opportunity in education, but if you come from a family that doesn't begin to know how to help their children to work hard at school and get to university, your chances must be reduced a hundred times, even if you are intelligent. How can there be any real equality of opportunity, comprehensive, or any other scheme educationalists choose to adopt, when a child's intelligence by the time he gets to school at the age of six, has already been very largely determined by its environment and the sort of intellectual stimulus it has received from its parents? Ignorance perpetuates itself.

For all the packing jobs we did, we were forced to concentrate most of the time just enough for it to be difficult to think about anything much else. But when there is time what do people think about? At Lucas's Carla would plan her new married life, while Dulcie looked back sadly on hers. They rhythmically flicked through the same plans and memories day after day. At the cake bakery the work was too hard and vile to allow the mind to work at all.

'You know what I think about at work?' said one woman. 'I win £50,000 every day.' She was packing canisters of Vim into cardboard boxes as she spoke. 'I redecorate my whole house from top to bottom and I go on three world cruises. And when I've spent it once in the first hour, I spend it all over again in the next. Sometimes I buy a house in London, sometimes a house in Majorca.'

Everywhere I went I was working with people who had missed any slight opportunity they might have had, or imagined they had, of changing their way of life, of getting out, of making it. Most of the people I was working with already had children who were too old to make the grade. Their children might still be able though, to dream of being pop stars, or being spotted by a Hollywood film director, avidly reading in magazines about people who had 'made it' in some utterly unlikely way. But for their tired middle aged parents, there was only one fantasy left, the big win on the football pools.

'If I won the pools,' everyone says at least once a day. Always 'If I won', never 'if I win'. No one really expects it. After all the chances are about one in a million, the worst odds a gambler could find. Most of the people who do the pools spend five shillings a week or more on them. It isn't even a very cheap fantasy.

A collector came round every Friday night to take the coupons and the money. The collectors get a commission on the money they take, but no wages. They collect on behalf of an area concessionaire who is paid by the firm. One Thursday night Mr Parkin, in whose house I was lodging, explained to me how to enter the pools. I was amazed at the complexity of the whole operation. He did the Littlewoods pools, and he gave me a booklet about it. Here were lists of different 'Full-perms' and 'Lit-Plans', very difficult to understand, and the booklet never quite explained. Beside each entry you have to write out something like 'Two entries of Lit-Plan 80 = 120 lines at 1p = 50p.' The number of spoiled entry forms sent in a week doesn't bear thinking about. It has to be exactly right. Mr Parkin was full of stories he'd heard of people doing the pools for twenty years, and finally thinking they'd won a fortune, only to discover that their entry wasn't valid, and none of their previous ones had been either. The company doesn't tell you if you consistently send up coupons with mistakes. You never discover until you think you've won. And worse, the company doesn't inform the winners. They have to write in within three days.

The booklet is scattered liberally with the grinning faces of people who have won immense amounts, Mrs Rolland of Potters Bar who won £200,442, Percy Harrison of East Stockwith who won £331,196. And on the last page of all, under the headline 'What £500,000 could mean to you! A luxury home . . . The car of your dreams . . . a fabulous holiday' is written, 'Have you any idea what a sum like £500,000 really means? Even after you've enjoyed a bumper spending spree and made provisions for your whole family's future, you could live in luxury for the rest of your life on the interest from your investments alone without ever touching a further penny of the capital!' The fantasy is played out to the last detail. 'Littlewoods do not regard their part as finished once you've received your big cheque. A special panel of experts is available to give you, if you wish, advice on every aspect of investment, setting up in business, house purchase, establishing funds for your family, income tax relief and many other financial matters.' It is made to look as solid as possible. If I subscribed to the conspiracy theorists' view of life I would say that the football pools were a perfect invention for giving the workers a perpetual carrot to dangle in front of their noses to keep them contented with their lot. In fact, I suppose, distasteful though it seems to me, it's a harmless dream that gives a bit of pleasure.

It was Mr Parkin's one indulgence. He spent the whole of Thursday night examining the teams' form and carefully marking in his X's on the coupon. All week he would study the football pages carefully, choosing his teams and changing his mind. He sent in a coupon for a syndicate he had organized with the people he worked with, as well as his own entry. He spent about ten shillings a week. He had once, over all those years, won sixteen shillings.

Mr and Mrs Parkin were in their late fifties and had lived in the village since they were married. Mr Parkin had been brought up there, and as a boy he went to the village school. He had worked for Lever Bros. all his life in the soapery. They rented the four-bedroomed house from the company, having moved from a smaller one when they had several children. Now their children had grown up and left home, they let out rooms. The only other lodger there at the time was a man hired by the dredging contractors who were working on Port Sunlight dock.

The village was built at the end of the century on a piece of marshy derelict land and one felt the marsh had never quite been reclaimed. All the houses in the village were said to be damp, and this was the dampest house I had ever been in. In my room the curtains were wet all the time, and it smelt so strongly of wet and mould that when the lights were out one could imagine mushrooms blossoming out of the cracks in the walls. All the houses had been built with bathrooms, but with outside lavatories. The Parkins a few years ago had decided to remedy this by partitioning off part of the room I was in with a piece of hardboard and putting the lavatory in this small space. The head of the bed leant against the partition and you could hear not just the flushing of the lavatory but the snap of elasticated knickers, the crinkle of lavatory paper.

The Parkins were an extremely respectable family. Neither of them had a Liverpool accent; they spoke in a soft indeterminate voice. They came, I later discovered, from non-conformist families, and although their background was purely working class, their attitudes and their whole way of life was very markedly middle class. He was a worker in the soapery earning an average wage, but they both voted Conservative and always had done. Later, when I spent some time in Rotherham I discovered from a shop steward that most of the miners who contracted out of the political levy to the Labour Party and, presumably, voted Conservative, were non-conformists. This is curious, as traditionally non-conformists have tended to vote Labour, and Catholics to vote Conservative.

Mr Parkin was a terse man who was tired most of the time he was at home. He had to be at work at half past seven every morning and he did an hour and a half overtime every day, so he didn't get back until about half past six in the evening.

'Father,' she said, 'is a great believer in the village. I think you have to be born here to accept it. At least we are near the edge and I can look out of my window and see the main road outside. But I couldn't live right in the middle. I'd go out of my mind. It isn't just that it's a dead place with nothing happening, it's because it belongs to the firm. Everything belongs to them, every bit of grass and breath of air.' She put down her crocheting and looked out of the window. 'There are other women here feel the same way. No one living in Bebington will come near the place. All the new people that come and live in it come from a long way away and they haven't grown up with the feeling against it that there is round here.'

Very few of the women I was working with lived in the village and those who didn't hated the idea. Mrs Parkin who had lived there since she married, had never got used to it.

Apart from more outdoor space, the village now has not got anything very special to offer its inhabitants, as it did in the old days. The rent is cheaper, but the houses are not necessarily more comfortable than the houses surrounding it. The amenities in the village are run down and dusty; the girls' club, the men's club, the various sports clubs, the Philharmonic society, the boys' brigade, and all those other leisure activities that suffer from the heavy hand of faded high-minded educational ideals, the sort of thing that people feel they ought to write down on questionnaires about hobbies. There is no cinema. The amateur dramatic society puts on shows from time to time. There is no Bingo hall, and there are no shops, except for one tiny post office. There is an open air swimming bath and a bowling green, and one pub, the Bridge Inn, which is closed on Sundays. People who want a drink usually go to the Brown Cow outside the village, and the Bridge Inn is an empty melancholy place. The Lever Club is a sort of working men's club where women can go, and where you can get a drink.

'It's a mausoleum,' Freda said, as I was working with her one afternoon. 'You've got to be dead to live in the village.' This was the general reaction to it, but there was as well a deeper and very understandable feeling of dislike. 'When you've got a job like this, you want to forget all about it when you go home, if you can. You don't want to rent your house from the firm, and be surrounded by the same faces you work with. If you live in the village you never get away. Your work is the whole of your life, and I couldn't stand that,' Freda said. 'Of course when my Dad was a boy it was different. There weren't many jobs or many houses, so they didn't mind. He spent half his time doffing his cap to the managers who lived in the village, or giving votes of thanks to the Viscount. On Sundays sometimes the Viscount would order a parade through the village with the Sunday school and the band, and he'd march at the head. Everyone had to come out on their doorsteps to watch.' I heard a great many other people talking about the village with the same kind of suspicion and distaste.

It is worth recording here that Lever Brothers are very good employers. They really do compare favourably with other firms of the same size throughout the country.

It is also worth recording the history of the village. It throws some light on why it is resented and disliked, although the houses there are probably still better to live in than many of those in the surrounding town, with the grass, and gardens and space for children to play. (There is a waiting list for houses in the village, but mostly, I was told, of people who have only recently arrived in the area.) There are still a great many people in Bebington who have lived there all their lives, who would never have anything to do with the village. Technically it is now owned and managed by another company, a subsidiary of Unilever, and is not directly attached to the factory. But most of the people who lived there weren't really aware of this. It's all 'Lever's' to them.

William Lever (later Viscount Leverhulme) was an extraordinarily forceful and determined man, almost a monomaniac. He had built up the firm from a small grocery business owned by his father. They were a strict nonconformist family and teetotallers. Having been the first to think of shredding soap into soap flakes, William Lever built up the grocery business into a soap factory at Warrington in Lancashire. But facilities there were cramped and he decided to move the factory to an entirely new area, where there would be room to build and expand as the company grew. He wanted a place big enough to build an empire of his own, where he would create houses for new workers to people his kingdom.

Of the site he chose, W.L. George, in his 'Labour and Housing at Port Sunlight' (published 1910) wrote, 'Anything more unprepossessing than this site can hardly be imagined. It was mostly but a few feet above high water level and liable at any time to be flooded by high tides and thus to become indistinguishable from the muddy foreshores of the Mersey . . . It did not at first sight seem fitted for human settlement.' But soap making being so dependent on raw materials, the advantages of water where a free dock could be built, and a railway line that ran right across the site, outweighed the difficulties.

Once the dock and the soapery was built Lever set about building houses for the workers. He thought of himself as an 'enlightened capitalist'. He was not, as he himself said, a philanthropist. 'There could be no worse friend to Labour,' he said in 1909, 'than the benevolent, philanthropic employer who carries his business on in a loose lax manner showing "kindness" to his employees . . . Sooner or later he will be compelled to close.'

He believed that a happy and contented work force would boost productivity. He also believed that if the workers were given an incentive, in the form of some kind of share in the firm's profits, they would be more likely to work harder. He was particularly interested in housing for workers, being a fervent and idealistic capitalist who saw that the social conditions of the urban worker were an indictment of the capitalist system.

Lever set about examining the various forms of profit-sharing that had been tried by numerous employers. None of them had worked at all well, or lasted for over five years. A few miles away Prices Candles had built a village, in Bromborough and the Bournville garden city was already in existence. This was the sort of project he decided to embark on. In his own words, in an interview in 1905, Lever said, 'If I were to follow the usual mode of profit sharing, I would send my workmen and work girls to the cash office at the end of the year and say to them, "You are going to receive eight pounds each; you have earned this money, it belongs to you. Take it and make whatever use you like of your money." Instead of that I told them, "Eight pounds is an amount which is soon spent and it will not do you much good if you send it down your throats in the form of bottles of whisky, bags of sweets or fat geese for Christmas. On the other hand, if you leave this money with me, I shall use it to provide for you everything which makes life pleasant, – viz. nice houses, comfortable homes and healthy recreation. Besides, I am disposed to allow profit sharing under no other than that form."'

The Unions hated the project from the start. Lever was setting up in the twentieth century, a feudal system in his empire, more rigid than any in the middle ages – the workers didn't even have their own strips to farm.

But he believed he was doing good and considered the interests of the workers and the employers to be synonymous. He wanted to 'build houses in which our work people will be able to live and be comfortable – semi-detached houses with gardens back and front, in which they will be able to know more about the science of life than they can in a back slum, and in which they will learn that there is more enjoyment in life than in the mere going to and returning from work and looking forward to Saturday night to draw their wages.'

Two types of cottage were built, the Parlour type having a big living room and a bedroom more than the Kitchen type. Every house had a bathroom, but not an inside lavatory. But it was the bizarre architectural style that caused most stir in the outside world. 'Two cottages are actually reproductions of Shakespeare's cottage at Stratford on Avon with great nooks and corners and fascinating gables' one observer enthused.

The Port Sunlight school had five hundred workers' children attending. Girl workers, of whom there were always a great number at the factory, had classes in cookery, dressmaking, shorthand and such at the Village Institute. Male workers' amenities were in the Gladstone Hall (so called because Gladstone opened it). But the rents in the village were not particularly low. People paid between a quarter and a fifth of their weekly wage, much the same as the average rent-payer in England expects to spend today.

Recreation for leisure time was provided by public institutions, a theatre, a concert hall, library, gymnasium, open-air swimming bath, men's club and societies for literature, music and art.

But Lever was a paternalist. 'The private habits of an employee,' he said, 'have really nothing to do with Lever Bros. providing the man is a good workman. At the same time, a good workman may have a wife of objectionable habits, or he may have objectionable habits himself, which make it undesirable to have him in the village . . . it is not a matter of a man being dismissed from his employment but merely being granted or refused a house in the village.'

In the winter at the weekly dances girls over the age of eighteen could 'submit the names of men to the social department which issues invitations to them unless there be reasons which militate against them'. A very short time after the village was founded, central management took over the control of the tenants' front gardens. People had been using their gardens for chicken runs, 'while,' said Lever, 'the family washing was unblushingly exposed on the railings'.

A church was built which was Congregational, and to put a stop to any religious disputes, Lever insisted that all services were to be strictly non-denominational, which worked to a point. However the vicar was heard to say, 'I sometimes feel that I am intended to be an advertisement for Sunlight Soap more than for the Kingdom of God.'

Resentment in the village grew and showed itself in various ways. In 1922 a branch of Macfisheries was opened in the village. Lever had just acquired the Macfisheries company. The villagers refused to buy at the shop, as they felt that the firm was trying to dictate to them how they should spend their money.

In a letter to Lever, the Secretary of the Bolton Branch of the Engineers Union wrote, 'No man of an independent turn of mind can breathe for long the atmosphere of Port Sunlight. That might be news to your Lordship, but we have tried it. The profit-sharing system not only enslaves and degrades the workers, it tends to make them servile and sycophant, it lowers them to the level of machines tending machines.'

As Lever Brothers grew and expanded out of Port Sunlight, and attached other subsidiary companies to itself, Lever decided to adopt a profit sharing system that would apply to all workers, and not just those at Port Sunlight. He adopted a scheme very like the ones he had at first rejected. He called it Copartnership, and it was meant to increase the sense of common interest between the three components of industry, capital, labour and management. The directors of Lever Bros. were to be the trustees of the Co-partnership trust. As, at the time, Lever himself was the only Ordinary share holder, this was a simple system to operate, and for all its names and ideals, amounted to no more than Lever handing out a small bonus to his workers, in the way that nearly all firms do, and did then too. But this bonus was only given on certain conditions.

Instead of shares, the employers were handed out Co-partnership certificates which were non-transferable and of no money value, but entitled them to an annual dividend. The employees were divided into four classes, Directors, Management, Salesmen and Staff. No one class could receive more than a quarter of the certificates issued. All co-partners were to be over twenty-five and to have been in service for five years.

In return for the certificates, the co-partners had to sign a document binding each 'not to waste time, labour, materials or money in the discharge of his duties, but loyally and faithfully to further the interests of Lever Brothers and its associated companies and his fellow co-partners to the best of his skill and ability'. If a co-partner were found guilty of neglect of duty, dishonesty, intemperance, immorality, wilful misconduct, flagrant inefficiency, disloyalty to his employers or any breach of his undertaking, his certificates could be cancelled.

The dividends paid out little. The average payment in 1912 was twenty pounds, but allowing for the directors' certificates, the majority of the co-partners received something nearer to thirty shillings on an annual income of £100. The scheme cost Lever's own pocket about £40,000 a year but he felt he would get it back on improved efficiency.

When there was a minor strike in the Oil Mill at Port Sunlight, Lever wrote that it was 'an opportunity to bring forward the relationship of co-partners to the firm at such times as a strike so that we may have a precedent created for future reference should any serious situation arise in the future when we may require the position of co-partners to be clearly defined'. That year a number of co-partnership certificates were granted for help given during the strike.

The system never really caught on. The co-partnership scheme was dropped finally in 1925. The village was later separated from the rest of the company and the whole profit sharing scheme was abandoned in favour of bonuses and pension schemes.

It was a scheme likely to fail. While intending to increase

productivity by making the workers happier, Lever had, according to the unions of the time, made them more resentful of the firm.

If anything is to be done to make life better for the workers only the state can improve their lives as a right and not as a gift with conditions and strings attached.

Chapter Seven

# Labour

The long benches with their dented and worn seats were half full. In that setting any group of people would have looked bedraggled and depressed. The old cream paint on the walls had faded to a deeper yellow, and the posters advertising the great life to be had in the forces were curling at the corners. The grinning faces in uniform beaming down from the walls looked unconvincing. This was a Yorkshire Employment Exchange on a cold Monday afternoon in March.

At the desk was a long row of cubicles with an Employment officer sitting in each. After waiting half an hour or so, the people on the benches were called up to the cubicles one by one.

'*Next please*!' called the officer in one cubicle. A big man in a cap and a blue workman's jacket came up to the desk and placed his large meaty hands on the lino top. You could tell his trade by his brown-red weatherbeaten face and the little pit marks in the skin. He worked in steel as an inspector in the melting shop, probing the molten metal to test its quality, exposed all day to sparks and gobbets of steel. For twenty years he had worked at the same job in the same steel works and was in his forties. Then suddenly he was fired for fighting with another man, and now he had been out of work for eight months.

'I'm not one of your layabouts on the Labour,' he said aggressively, 'I'm not one of your shirkers on charity.'

'Mr Williams,' said the officer firmly, 'We don't seem to be very successful in finding you a job. Now tell me, have you considered re-training?'

'Oh yes, they talked that one at me last week, and they weren't very sociable,' said the man, boiling up to a rage with startling speed. 'They threatened to change my classification, and they can't do that to me.'

The officer took a deep breath and tried to keep his temper. 'Mr Williams,' he said slowly, 'it is in your interest to lower your classification if you haven't been able to find a job within a reasonable time.'

'But I'm an inspector,' said the man. 'When all's said and done, I'm an inspector, and I worked my way up to it.' He brought one of his great fists down on the desk. 'You can't put me down as a general labourer. I'll do temporary labouring if you like, but I won't have you change my classification.' He leant across the desk to the officer and said, 'And there's no privacy here either. Everyone can hear through the partition, and I won't have them hearing me being put down as a general labourer.' He leant back in his chair again and said, 'I don't like it on the Labour, you know.'

'Then why not retrain?' said the officer, reaching for a brochure on training schemes.

'I'm used to twenty-two pounds a week. I won't get that if I train, will I?' he said. They'd been through all this before.

'Well, you'd have to make sacrifices during that six months, of course,' said the officer, with an air of deliberate patience. 'But we'll make you from a semi-skilled to a skilled man, with a great deal more earning potential at the end of it.'

The man listened suspiciously. While he was training he would get £11.50 a week clear to keep his wife and child. He'd be under no obligation, would be taken on a tour of the college, meet his instructors first, and he'd find out what goes on.

'This,' said the officer, 'is the welfare state, and this is a benefit for you.' But the officer's voice was not as convincing as it might have been. He didn't sound as if he thought there was a chance of the man accepting. The man was not slow to notice the dryness of tone and to take offence at it.

'The state will spend £800 on your six-month course,' said the officer. 'Look at it from their point of view. The powers that be take a look at you and say to themselves, "Why is this capable and able-bodied man out of work?" Before the officer had time to finish, the other fist came down on the table, 'Why don't the powers that be talk about my twenty years work in steel then? They forget about that quick enough, don't they, eh?'

Nothing was resolved there and then. It was put off for another week while the man went away with a fist full of brochures to think about retraining. Otherwise, the officer made it clear, if he turned down the course, next week he would have to reconsider being reclassified. A man cannot be reclassified immediately by an officer. If he has been on the dole a long time and still disputes his classification, the case is taken to the supervisor who makes the final decision.

'A sad case,' said the officer, putting away the man's file. 'A man stays in one job for a good many years, and when he loses that, he can't seem to get settled anywhere else. He'd really like to be back in the same job with his old mates and he doesn't want to work anywhere else. It happens quite often, a typical case. He's been unlucky. Says he'll work anywhere, but he's far too choosy. Been out of work for eight months. He's well into the rhythm of unemployment now. No one wants to take on men who've been out that long. Training? He won't touch it. I'll have to consider him for reclassification next week and now he's had his six months, he'll lose his earnings related benefit and have to go on to social security. He's not an easy man and he'll never get back into work that he likes. He won't work much again.'

The man was ambling out of the door, his thick strong neck hunched in his jacket, hands clenched in his pocket. A bit of bad luck, one fight at work after twenty years, and this tough hard-working man was thrown off his balance. His pride had taken a beating and now he was feeling like a bear being bated by the hounds of bureaucracy and tight-lipped officialdom – a big solid man bursting with impotent directionless fury.

'Next, to cubicle 7, *please*!' called the officer. A clean young boy in a soft blue jersey and a bovver jacket came up and sat down.

'I'm sorry,' said the officer kindly, 'we still haven't come up with anything.' The boy looked resigned. He was eighteen and had served two and a half years of an apprenticeship. The firm had suddenly transferred leaving him and fifteen other apprentices still holding on to their useless articles and contracts. The

Exchange was having trouble in finding someone to take them on half way through their apprenticeship. No-one was keen to employ eighteen year olds at £11.95 minimum when they could get sixteen year olds cheaper. He had a list of ten firms that he had already tried. The officer had to send him away and tell him to go on hoping. 'Isn't the firm liable?' I asked. 'Aren't apprenticeship articles legally binding?'

'They were a good firm,' said the officer. 'But when it comes down to it the men, the apprentices, all the employees in any firm are just names on the clock to be hired and fired by head office decision in London. That boy didn't have a chance. There was nothing I or anyone else could do.'

Next there was the engineer who had just started on a new job and wanted to move.

'They said at the interview I'd be getting three more pounds a week than they gave me. The other men there said, "Oh, they always promise more than they pay." Well, the wife's having a baby. I need the money.'

The officer found him another job. The man was skilled and it was easy.

Then there was the foreman in a saw-making shop who'd been in one job for twelve years. He couldn't find work anywhere. 'I don't think he'll work much again,' said the officer. 'He's a good man, but no one wants an old foreman from another firm.'

Next in the line was an Indian fork and spoon polisher who had hit a minor slump in fork and spoon polishing. Then came a man who had been out of work for five years, and he was angry.

'I'm a good electrician, so why can't I get work?' he demanded.

'It's very difficult, you know,' said the officer quietly. 'But we'll go on paying.' But that wasn't enough. It wasn't money he wanted.

'I want work,' he said. The officer was kind, but got rid of him quickly. 'He's mentally disabled, I'm afraid,' he explained to me, 'but he won't accept it. He can't work. Sometimes he comes in here so quietly. If he sees a new officer, they often don't know about him and give him jobs. He gets thrown out almost at once. Causes no end of trouble at work. Some days he comes in here ready to tear the place apart. You know, we get a lot of them. I don't think many people realize how many there are. Many of them refuse to be registered, so there aren't statistics, but we get to know them.'

As the city has no employment problems, most of the people calling at the Employment Exchange were quickly found work. If they stayed on the books they were misfits, the unlucky ones who were either mentally or in some way emotionally unable to adjust themselves to work.

In another Northern city the space situation was altogether different. Unemployment there is so severe that men who actually didn't want to work were almost welcomed with open arms by the Employment officers. As well as the staggering dearth of unskilled jobs 200 apprenticeships had closed in the last few years. Unemployment breeds unemployment, and some whole families had been out of work since 1948. The area has a higher birth rate than the average, and because of the large proportion of big families, the workers there tend to be more immobile than workers in other parts of the country.

The Employment Exchange here is in a place like a huge old warehouse. A maze of partitions is set up in the building. It looks like a cattle market with pig-pens.

I sat in a cubicle and watched.

A black machine operator sat down and began to talk in a rapid gunfire of almost inaudible words. 'I hate being in the house all day. I don't like it. I want any factory job. I'm not married, but I have a woman.'

'I've only got one job, I'm afraid. On a capstan centre-lathe. Can you do that?'

'I don't know until I see the machine, but I hope so. I can't bear being at home all day any more,' he said.

'Well, I'll send you down for an interview to this job. They haven't notified me that it is filled, but I'm warning you, three men have already gone down there for an interview this morning. I doubt if it's still vacant.'

The man took a small green interview card with him and set off quickly. 'I don't think he'll get it,' said the officer. 'The employer can pick and choose and that man's English isn't good. I could hardly understand him, and I don't think the employer will bother to try.'

In the next door partition there was a row going on. A woman Employment officer was almost shouting, 'Well, you'll just have to get up in the morning, my boy. There are plenty of other people who catch a train and a bus to get to work. It isn't so very far you know. Do you know what time I get up to get to work? Six o'clock. Yes, six o'clock.'

The offices and cubicles and typing pools were divided only by thin walls. The great ceiling of the warehouse echoed with the sounds.

Another man came in and sat down. He too was black. He presented a rejection slip from a car firm to the officer. 'So you did go to the interview this time?' said the officer. The man, who looked tired and old, had bright red eye balls and he shifted around uncomfortably in his chair. He was an experienced deck-hand who didn't want to go back to sea. 'You've been out since December, haven't you? I'm afraid I shall have to suggest that the insurance people suspend your pay,' he said, with a genuine note of apology in his voice. 'You'll have to go on to social security. But I have got a job here that might do. What about signing on at the Pool? Well, there's a job in the next town being a deck hand on the ships in dock. Monday to Friday, £16.44 a week. How about that?'

The man was cracking his knuckles and looking down at the floor. 'That's a long way to go to work.'

'It's not so far. You've got to get used to the idea of travelling a bit. We can't all work on our front-door steps, you know.'

The man agreed to go for an interview. 'He doesn't want work at the moment,' said the officer when he'd gone. 'He got a bad discharge from his last ship. He might go back to sea when it's blown over. He wouldn't think of going all that way to work.'

Next came a peach faced boy with a ginger jacket, and red braces.

'This is the first time you've signed on?' asked the officer.

'I'm eighteen. I was at the youth place before,' he explained. As he talked he rested both hands on the table in front of him. On one finger was a gold signet ring which he twisted round and round.

'What have you done since you left school?'

'I worked for two months in a factory. Then I went as a boy soldier in the army, but I left after nine months. I couldn't stick it. So I went back to my first job, but only stayed three months. Then I did bill posting for a year, and I was made redundant. I was in a venetian blind factory after that. I did a bit of labouring once too.'

'Six jobs since you left school? Not a very good record.'

'I went down to the buses yesterday to see if they'd train me as a driver, but they don't take eighteen year olds. I want a job that'll teach me to drive. I nearly can. On the bill posting job they were teaching me, but then I was made redundant just before the test and I didn't have a car to do the test in.'

'Have you been taking lessons since then?'

'Lessons? No, they're too expensive.'

'But if you really want to learn, it would be worth making sacrifices, wouldn't it?'

'But I want a job where they'll teach me.'

'Well, it seems to me that you haven't been trying very hard for yourself. You can't have everything given to you on a plate. I know I can't find a job that'll teach you. You go away and learn. I might find you something then. You see,' he said flicking through the file of cards on his desk, 'there's only one driving job at the moment – a dairy job, loading and driving. They don't want to muck about teaching you.' The boy shrugged, and then nodded.

'Now, until you learn to drive, will you take a job in a car factory?'

'Oh no, they're always on strike.'

'How far will you travel?'

'Only in this town. But today I'm going round building sites to try and get myself a job labouring,' he said. The officer leant back in his chair.

'I don't reckon much on your chances of success,' he said. 'You have to know someone who knows someone in that trade. You need someone to introduce you to the foreman or you'll get a pretty cool reception.'

'Well, my sister works at the electrics factory. She could find me something, but it's bad there.'

'Look, would you be interested in training?'

'Training? No. Only as a driver.'

As this was his first week on the dole, they left it at that. 'I'd guess he doesn't want to work at all,' said the officer. 'Maybe he can be persuaded to take driving lessons while he's on the dole.' There was no pressure to make him work. Save the jobs for the ones who need them. Giving out a job was more like granting a benefit than giving out the dole.

Now, during the last election, a number of M.P.'s noted that one of the main causes for the swing to the Tories was hatred of the idea that somehow somewhere there was a large group of 'shirkers' living on the dole and social security. The newspapers at the time were so busy writing about who would be in Mr Wilson's new cabinet, that they ignored some of the shouting that was going on at the meetings. Everywhere there was a man who would say he knew someone who knew someone who had a friend who was drawing twenty-five pounds a week on the Labour and had been for the last five years, because he didn't much fancy working. The layabouts, the no-goods, the spongers on public charity. This is one of the extraordinary myths that build up from nowhere. Like the story that if you earn over a certain amount you begin to be taxed more than you earn and end up paying something like twenty-five shillings in the pound. With unemployment figures at their highest for a long time the notion of the 'shirkers' becomes almost cruel.

The problem of unemployment is complex. It breeds a mentality of dependence on the state, resistance to the values of society, and in particular, a lack of any feeling that work is intrinsically good. I have already pointed out that unemployment tends to run in families. Where the father hasn't worked in years, the son has no special incentive to do so. Mass unemployment over a long stretch of time makes for mass unemployability. Now to turn on these feckless and wretched boys and accuse them of shirking because they aren't trying at all, even though at their age they might well find it, isn't in any real sense justified.

The men who know about all this best are the Employment officers. In neither city that I went to did I find one officer who considered that there were people living on the dole out of idleness and desire to cadge off the state. This was not because it would have wounded their professional pride to admit to the existence of a large number of shirkers – they are eager enough to discuss the shortcomings of their work and the limitations of their power. It was because day after day and year after year they were dealing with people face to face they had some fairly clear insight into their lives. If someone was out of work for a long time, there was always a reason, and the reason was either environmental or mental inability to adjust, the two problems often being inseparable.

The next man to make his way into the cubicle was a huge tough sailor with a smashed-in face and a bent-up ear. His hands were fat and cracked with dirt and his tufty hair was dyed a metallic peroxide auburn, and his neck and wrists were tattooed. His clothes were shabby and blotched with stains, and he was in a bad mood.

'I'm not coming here to sign on the dole,' he said. 'I'm on my holiday pay at the moment and I want a job as soon as that's used up.'

'What sort of job?' asked the officer a little nervously.

'I'm a chef, a trained chef and confectioner. I can do butchery too. Now I want a job without split duties. I want to start in the morning and end in the evening. No messing around with six in the morning till three in the afternoon and then six at night till one in the morning.'

The officer seemed to be finding it as hard as I was to imagine this man as a chef.

'Excuse my asking, but as you haven't signed on before, have you got your City and Guilds qualification? I mean, what I'm really asking, is why you weren't sent to the hotel and catering section? That's our special section that deals with the trade.'

The man bristled and puffed out his cheeks. 'I been there already and they said they had nothing for me, and I'd better come down to you and see what you could do for me. Now don't think I don't know what's going on, because I do. Now I'll tell you this,' he said and leant across the table to shake a finger in the officer's face. 'I'm a proper trained chef. Fully trained, and I've served my time at it, without your tests and qualifications. I was a cook before I went in the navy, I was a cook in the navy and was a cook in the war. I've worked in nearly every hotel and restaurant from one end of this city to the other. I've worked in the Grand as a chef too. Now you just pick up that blasted phone and ask them. I've done passenger boats from here to Timbuctoo and I can cook any dish. You name it, I can cook it. You can't name it? I'll still cook it.' He leant back and looked defiant.

'Well,' said the officer, anxious to get rid of him. 'I might be able to find you canteen or hospital work with fixed hours. I can't guarantee it would be a chef's job though. I'll see what I can do.'

'You just do that,' said the man, rising to his feet and propping himself up on the table. 'But remember I'm a fully trained chef, and a bloody good one too.' He stomped away, and the officer took out a handkerchief and mopped his forehead slowly.

'He's probably a bit unbalanced. Anyway no one would take him as a chef. He's not qualified and just look at him. I must admit, I thought he was going to get a bit stroppy.'

In the next door box was a derelict old man, who had been waiting for an officer quietly. Half asleep with his elbows resting on the desk, he looked down and out, and was blearily thumbing through some leaflets about the army. The officer got up and went into the next cubicle, 'Thinking of joining up mate?' he laughed kindly. The man gazed at him and sat up straight. 'Anything for me this week?' he asked. 'Sorry. Nothing. Here's your card,' said the officer. The man dragged himself to his feet, touched his ragged forelock and crept away.

Then a strange grey face appeared round the door, with huge eyes and a grin. 'So sorry, Sir!' he said and withdrew quickly. The officer shrugged.

A boy in blue denim dungarees came in. He'd been a boy soldier, but had left and was working as a production operator at the car works. He now wanted day work and didn't want to do shifts. 'I'm not asking for money,' he said. 'I've got ninety pounds put aside. I just want a better job. You don't know what it's like on shifts.' The officer said he would do what he could but things weren't looking good in that line. He turned to me and said, 'The trouble with people here is that they won't travel any distance to work, and they won't work shifts. These things always go by tradition. They have an easy working tradition here. They don't want their lives mucked around by their work.'

I asked about the army, as two boys had been boy soldiers who came that day. 'Oh yes, a few local boys join up. Not many stay.' With the army having such severe recruiting difficulties, was there any pressure on him to try and persuade people to join up? 'Oh they try it a bit. They send us all this stuff and sometimes they talk to us about it. But really, their recruiting problems are not our business.'

The door opened and a sharply dressed man bounced in, leant across the desk and patted the officer on the arm, with a laugh. The officer laughed and said, 'Hello. How are you?' Another officer came in to say 'Hello' as well. 'Things are good, just very good,' said the man, still laughing. He was a particularly beautiful half caste with longish curly hair. 'So how's the wife?' asked the officer who had just come in. 'Oh fine, fine,' said the man.

'Now tell me,' said the officer interviewing, 'did you get the job you went for yesterday?' The man threw his hands in the air and with a joke gesture and shrugged, 'Man, they didn't want me.' Both officers laughed. 'You know,' said the one standing up, 'when it comes to job-hunting, this fellow has skates under him. He went for two jobs the other day, and was out and back in under half an hour!' They all laughed again. The man had such charm, it was easy to see why they all liked him. 'He's one of our best customers!' and they laughed again. Finally they found another job for him to try, this time as a warehouseman. The man took the card and breezed away, with a wave and a joke or two.

'He never gets a job,' said the officer. 'Although he's so nice and good. You see, he has a very bad stammer indeed. You wouldn't think it to see him here with us, but when he first came here it was dreadful. We didn't know what to do. It took half an hour to get one word out, and then he has quite a strong accent. He's got to know us now, and it hardly ever happens here, but when he goes for the interviews, he can hardly say a word. Very sad. He really wants work, and it would give him confidence. We do explain to employers before they see him that when he settles down he'll soon stop stammering, but they don't believe it when they see him. They won't give him a chance.'

Later I went over to the female Employment officer dealing with hotel and catering vacancies. She looked like a hotel manageress herself.

A seedy looking woman with a shiny face was called up to the table from the benches.

'I want to go away, you see, for the Easter season,' she said. She was in her early forties and looked run down. 'I'm a kitchen maid, at the school up the road.'

'The mentally handicapped school? How long have you been there?'

'Three years. Now I want a change. I'd go for a kitchen-maid or a chambermaid. I want to be in Blackpool.'

'Have you been here before?' asked the officer.

'Oh no, I usually go to the private agencies, but they're so expensive.'

'I see. Well, I'll look and see what we've got out of town.' She thumbed through a file of index cards on her desk. 'Ah yes, Keswick. How would a kitchen-maid in Keswick do?'

'Where's that then?'

'That's in the Lake District,' said the officer, 'very beautiful.'

'Lake District? Oh no. That's all full of coloured students.'

'I've never heard that,' said the officer looking surprised.

But the woman was shaking her head vigorously so she didn't pursue it.

'Look, I'm afraid everyone wants to go to Blackpool. There just isn't anything for you there. Would you consider something nearer here?'

'Well, if that's all there is. I had wanted to go away, like. Somewhere by the sea.'

'I'm sorry. There really isn't anything else. Now, do you have your own black and white? You'll be doing some chambermaid duties and you have to provide your own.'

'Yes, that's all right. But it is living in, is it? I live in at the school, you see. I'm not married or anything.'

She went away reasonably contented. But the officer doubted whether she'd get the job.

A tough looking fat boy came and sat down next. He splayed his padded fingers across his round knees, and screwed up his features as he spoke. He handed his cards across the table without saying a word, and the officer went to find his file. When she came back he began,

'I'm a waiter. Been in the trade six years.' As he spoke he showed that he had almost no teeth, although he was only twenty-two. 'I'm an experienced barman too.'

The officer was perusing his file. 'Oh yes,' she said slowly, and drew a long breath. 'I remember you now. I'm afraid we haven't anything for you.' But before she had finished he interrupted, 'Now don't start telling me to go down to the Labour again and sign on as a general worker. They've nothing for me there in my line. I'm a waiter.'

The officer pursed her lips and stared him right in the eye. 'You've had so many jobs from here, that they don't bear counting. There is nothing for you here.'

'Right then, I'll complain. I'm complaining to the union. I'll complain to your boss. I'll be back,' and he got up and went straight out of the door.

'He's no waiter,' said the officer crossly when he'd gone. 'Look, just look at his record. He hasn't held down one job for more than two days. He never had training and he can't do the job. The employers don't want us to keep sending them duds. They lose faith in us, and start going to all the private agencies. That's bad for all the people who come to us who *are* good.'

Now this is a problem that dogs the whole Employment Exchange system. 'The Labour' still has a bad image and employers tend to assume that anyone who is sent to them from there must be hopeless. Many will not interview men from the Employment Exchange and persist in believing that they will get better applicants from private agencies, small-ads, or by word of mouth amongst the workers themselves. 'Applicants from the Labour,' they will say, 'don't really want work. They just want you to sign their card and turn them down so that they can get the dole.' Or, 'if they had any initiative they wouldn't expect to be spoon-fed with jobs by the state. They'd go out and find jobs for themselves.' Or 'They only turn to the Employment Exchange to help them get jobs when they've been turned down everywhere else.'

Of course this is only the attitude of some employers, but it is true of enough of them to make the work of the Employment officers that much harder. Some of the best workers have cottoned on to the fact and they keep away from the Exchange as they think it contaminates them in some way and diminishes their status and their chances of work. Also they think that the Exchange is a place you go to for casual unskilled work, and is not likely to offer the best jobs. Private agencies and advertisements have a sort of glamour, an image of offering the better jobs.

The Department of Employment does, of course, offer a service to everyone. It is also progressively rehousing its services in modern, central offices instead of in drab back-streets; generally giving them a facelift and often it is physically separating in different buildings the payment of unemployment benefits (which is such a drag on employment work) from the positive business of placing people in work.

But popular prejudice – and misguided notions about the Department of Employment – make for a situation where Employment officers are forced to be extremely careful in sending only the very best, and most obvious candidates to apply for better jobs. They can't give the benefit of the doubt to a man who doesn't look too promising, but with a bit of encouragement might shake down well in a job. An officer can't take risks of any kind. The haphazard selection of employees by many employers also means that they may well not be getting the men who are best for the job. An Employment officer could sift through all his clients and find the person who would best fit the job. The employer who resorts to advertising takes what comes and would have many less men to choose from.

A number of the Employment officers that I met, felt that Employment Exchanges should be given far more power, that they should at least be on an equal footing with the private agencies. But being so much poorer, they can't compete fairly. If most jobs were arranged by the Exchange, they feel, the system would work more efficiently and more fairly, both to employers and employees. There is no doubt that private agencies often cause tremendous harm, particularly amongst women clerical workers. It seems to me that they scoop off the very best secretaries and persuade them to keep changing jobs as often as possible. This means that employers can never get good secretaries who stay, the employers have to keep paying fair sized commissions to the agencies, and the non-agency secretaries tend to get the worst jobs. In time of full employment or in time of unemployment the officers feel, probably quite rightly, that they are by far the most qualified men to sort out the right people and the right jobs.

The natural objection to this would be that the employers would want to choose their men for themselves. But there is no reason why this wouldn't enable them to do so far more easily. Similarly, it could be said that the employees would have to trust entirely to the officers' assessment of their chances, but again, far more choice would be made available to them through this system. Already in one or two towns the Department of Employment has set-up 'Self-service' Exchanges, where all the jobs are posted on a board and anyone can select a vacancy and ask for an interview from the officer.

'But,' said one officer with a voice of resignation, 'they won't ever do anything dynamic about Employment Exchanges. Until they spend more money on changing the image of Employment Exchanges, the old attitude will remain and everyone would be shocked to think that people had to get their jobs compulsorily through them. Until then? Well, we'll muddle along as best we can.'

Chapter Eight

# Coal

In January the snow in Rotherham is black. It lies like old fungus on the roofs and streets. It isn't the worst place in England – it hasn't got the highest pollution, or the highest unemployment or the highest industrial disease or accident rate. There are a good many places that are worse. It's only designated as an Intermediate area by the government, not as a development area.

Nowadays Rotherham is almost a suburb of Sheffield. There's no way of knowing where Rotherham ends and Sheffield begins, and yet it does still have a distinct identity of its own. Traditionally it is a coal-mining and steel-producing town and, in spite of pit closures and 'rationalization' of both industries, leading to redundancies and increasing unemployment, no new industry of any importance has grown up there. The town council has made a report to the government stating that in ten years' time, if nothing is done, a quarter of Rotherham's male working population will be out of work.

Chronic bronchitis reaches a high level in the town. South and West Yorkshire has the worst bronchitis in the world. Down in the valley of the River Don and the Rother, a thick mist hangs over the town for much of the winter. When people there talk about the weather they often mean the smoke that belches out of the factory chimneys, and the way the wind is blowing. The smell of sulphur and other chemicals in parts of the town is overwhelming. The power station pours out half a ton of dust and grit and two tons of sulphur dioxide an hour. Steel Peech and Tozer, the main steel works, chokes out iron oxide, a thick red dust, and the Midland Iron Company and others add to the halo of grime and filth that hangs over the town. From the wild and bleak countryside that surrounds Rotherham on three sides, looking back on the town you can see the flat black clouds bearing down on it.

In and around the town there are large areas of derelict land; ground choked with small heaps of industrial waste, stagnant marshes, tips and notices threatening prosecution. The government offers 75 per cent grants for the reclamation of this ravaged land, but no-one seems anxious to take up the proposition.

Rotherham is the only place in Yorkshire and Humberside where the population, now 87,000, is dropping. The town council is worried that if new industry doesn't come soon, thousands more will leave.

Both mining and steel industries have strong traditions of their own, and the town has two quite closely knit communities.

Manvers is one of the twelve collieries in and around Rotherham, one of the nineteen that make up the South Yorkshire coal field. It employs 1,550 men. I was told it was quite a thin seam, but until I went down I didn't realize what that meant.

The miner who took me down was a tallish man in his late thirties, dead white, thin and boney. He carried a Davy lamp and a stick with a carved round top, and he had a pair of black rubber pads buckled to his knees. He was a deputy. 'A deputy,' he explained, 'deputizes for the management in the pit. We are responsible at law for anything that goes wrong.' Later talking about his job he said, 'You won't find many people working in factories and other industries who are made responsible for so much. It's not an enviable position.'

I was given a pair of overalls with 'N.C.B.' (National Coal Board) printed on them, a white helmet, and a pair of gum boots heavy enough for walking on the moon. A battery was fitted to a belt round my waist with a long lead to a light that could be held while walking, or fixed to the helmet. I was also given a heavy safety device, to fix to the belt. If there was a fire the machine would turn carbon dioxide into nitrogen so that you could breathe, at any rate for a while. I had to sign an indemnity for the Coal Board, 'Just in case we don't bring you up again,' one of the managers said.

At the top of the shaft there are two air lock doors and your ears pop as you go through them. Fresh air is sucked through the pit from the shaft at one end where the coal is taken out. A fan pulls the foul air out of the shaft which the miners use. We stood in the small cage surrounded by wire netting and were plummeted to the bottom of the pit, some 700 feet down. There was a rush of air coming up the shaft, and as the cage neared the bottom, sprays of dirty water shot up at us. On this particular day one of the pumps in the pit had gone wrong, and there was a lot of water underfoot.

Stepping out of the cage at the bottom of the shaft was like being on the platform of some run down London underground station late at night. There was a smell of dust and coal and urine. In a small brick walled office were a couple of men drinking tea, by a telephone to the surface, and a big clock. It was dimly, but adequately lit.

We set off down the tunnel, walking between railway tracks on uneven sleepers. There was electric light and the tunnel was big, about eight feet high and eight feet wide. After a hundred yards we came to a locomotive, a 'man-rider', with seats for passengers, and we were driven a mile, transferred to another train and driven another mile, all this time in the dark. We got out and the train disappeared back down the tunnel. There was only light from the torches we carried and the Davy lamp.

Now there was a walk of half a mile or so. The tunnel leading to the coal face was rough and small, and there was a good deal of water underfoot. The main tunnels had seemed so secure and regular that it was difficult to imagine cave-ins and roof-falls. They were smooth and high and supported every foot or so by strong steel arches. Here, in a minor gallery which would only be used for a limited amount of time, it didn't feel so safe. The corrugated iron between the steel arches bulged, the floor was jagged and uneven. At its highest it was only six feet high; mostly it was five feet or less. Where there was water it was dangerous to walk as we couldn't see where we were putting our feet, so we balanced along the tracks, holding on to the pipes on the ceiling. Walking in the dark is a good deal more tiring than walking in the light, and it seemed to take us a very long time. The pipes in the roof were draining poisonous methane out of the coal and at points in the main tunnels there was a great hiss of air, so loud you couldn't speak over it, as the gas was blown out to mix and be diluted with the current passing through. In this long dark gallery it was hot. 'Not so hot as most,' I was told. The temperature underground rises two degrees fahrenheit for every 100 feet down.

The deputy said, as we felt our way through the dark, 'You'll find a miner only feels safe in his own seam. He can hear the sounds in the roof and underneath him. He'll know what's safe and what isn't. Each seam has its own sounds and its own characteristics. Put a miner to work in a strange seam and he'll be scared as hell. Even if the conditions are far better in another seam, a man will fight as hard as he can not to be moved. This is a thin seam, but if you ask any of these men if they'd rather work a thick seam somewhere else, he'll say no. It would take him a month or much longer to get to know another one so that he felt safe in it.' This man had been a miner all his life, so had his father, and his father's father. Since becoming a deputy (the equivalent of a charge hand in a factory) he had joined the deputies' union. There are only two unions in mining. Everyone, other than deputies, whether he is an electrician or has any other special skill, belongs to the National Union of Mineworkers.

So far we had hardly seen any miners at all. The whole place seemed to be deserted. Then at last there was a dim light ahead in the distance. As we approached I saw it was a cluster of lights from men's helmets. At the end of the tunnel was a group of men squashed together. They were working at shoring up the sides and the roof and there was a barrier of stone at the end. The rails underfoot came to a stop and there was a truck waiting to carry coal or slag away from the face. I was surprised at the number of men working in the small space but it was as I had thought it would be. I thought this was all there was to see. 'Do you want to see the face?' one miner asked, when I thought that was what I was looking at. In a moment he had disappeared through a hole at the bottom of the wall. It was such a small hole that I hadn't noticed it; it looked more like a badger's burrow than a passage for fully grown men, being about eighteen inches high and the same in width. Getting down on his stomach, he squirmed his way in with slippery agility. One of the other men gave me a pair of knee pads and some rubber gloves, and with difficulty, I followed him into the face.

I could hardly believe what I saw in there. I thought the small entrance would widen out and I would find myself in something like a cave, but it didn't. The roof was about two and a half feet high. It was supported by hydraulic valve props set a foot apart in all directions. To move around you had to worm your way on your stomach in and out of the props. If you stopped and sat down, you had to sit with your head on your knees because there wasn't room to sit normally. The only lights in there were the torches on the miner's helmets, and there were about twelve men working in this tiny confined area. The tunnel was six feet wide running down the seam, which was 180 yards long. The miners work the whole 180 yards length of the seam going up and down, cutting out more coal each time. When I was there they happened to be working near the entrance but there would be times when they would have to crawl the entire length on their bellies before they even began work.

This was where I understood the difference between working a thick and a thin seam. The height of the roof at the coal face is determined by the thickness of the seam and you can't cut away more than that thickness to make working easier as it would make the roof unsafe.

The process of getting out the coal in this pit was done almost completely by the machine. The coal cutter operates on chains and shuttles up and down the face pulling out the coal in small bits. This sort of coal is used by industries and power stations. Imagine working in such a confined space, picking and shovelling for seven hours of an eight hour shift.

The coal is loosened first by blasting and it is this that causes by far the most accidents. There are rigid safety regulations laid down but even when these are carefully observed, it is easy for things to go wrong. The appalling conditions at the coal face can't really be made better. The Coal Board does what it can.

It isn't surprising that there is a lot of absenteeism among miners. At Manvers the general manager said that each miner only averaged four out of five shifts a week. There must be some days when the work seems unbearable, particularly getting out of bed at four in the morning, or setting out to work at nine at night. The 'Miners Monday' is a well known phrase in Rotherham, there being more men missing on a Monday than any other day.

'What's the weather like outside?' one miner asked us. 'Is it snowing again?' They'd begun their shift at five in the morning in the dark. We sat hunched up in a row, one or two of them having a few minutes' rest while the other worked. One of them asked me what I thought of it and I said that it seemed to me a terrible place to work. 'But this is a lot better than some,' he answered. 'Many pits aren't so mechanized.'

Until three years ago there were pit ponies at Manvers. The stables are still there, near the shaft, underground, and the ponies' names are still written up in the dark. There is a big poster on the wall showing a miner falling off a pony, with the words, 'It is dangerous to ride.' The deputy told me that in fact men used to sneak rides along the passages when no one was looking. The ponies would be brought to the surface on national holidays, but otherwise they lived all their lives in the pit. There are still 160 mines using ponies.

A miner's work couldn't be called boring. There is enough danger to create the tension you can sense all the time in the pit. There are a lot of jokes, and talking and laughing. At the coal face itself you can't but be afraid, with the walls and the roof pressing in on you. The space is so small that you feel as you crawl along that it would take such a tiny shift in the earth to be crushed instantly. You feel as vulnerable as a beetle that has miraculously escaped being crushed under foot by the arch in the sole of a boot. Only the small props separate you from millions of tons of rocks. With dust in your nose and throat and the thick smell of coal everywhere, the heat, the noise of the machinery, I felt that after hours in there it would be easy to panic.

Most miners will agree that mining is a terrible life and yet they are forced to fight as hard as they can against the closure of pits. They are like prisoners begging to be kept in prison to avoid starvation. Retraining, it is often said, is the great panacea to the miner's troubles. But in a place like Rotherham, massive training schemes on their own would hardly help. To retrain men haphazardly in the hope that new industry will come, is not much use. An industrialist, wondering whether to bring a new factory to the town will sound out existing skills, and the chances are that the men haven't been trained for the right thing. It's no use giving them all highly skilled training, when there aren't the jobs for them, unless they move away. There is one government retraining centre in Sheffield, but it is used mostly for rehabilitation of men who have been disabled.

I came up from the pit with the morning shift at one o'clock. Waiting for the cage to come down the miners were leaning against the walls at the bottom of the shaft, silent with exhaustion and black even to the insides of their eyelids. On the wall was a large notice signed by the general manager of the pit, telling the miners that they hadn't worked their quota of coal in the last year. The young boys of seventeen looked about twelve, with their faces blackened, and long tousled hair encrusted with coal dust. The cage came down and all squeezed in, standing in a line with our feet between two rails, holding on to a bar just above our heads. We shot up to the top, the air rushing at us in all directions, the sides of the shaft uneven, and dimly visible in the light from the torches on our helmets. The man next to me was humming and a couple of others joined in. They were humming an aria from 'La Traviata'.

Through the air lock doors again, and suddenly out into the cold January day; one has lost all sense of time and weather. The men are waiting to go down to start the next shift, taking a last drag on their cigarettes, a last look around at the day, as it will be night time when they come out. They pass ready-lit cigarettes to their friends on the retiring shift, who grasp them thankfully. Eight hours without a cigarette is quite a strain for a smoker. Taking matches into a pit is a very serious offence, punishable by prison. Sometimes the men are searched. In the pit most men chew tobacco as a substitute and a thirst quencher. Many take snuff.

The two shifts smile, exchange jokes, and the clean bright men, all of them pale, pass through the doors. The black and exhausted men make their way to the pithead baths. When they come out washed, looking clean and smart in their own clothes, you might think they had spent the morning in a light and airy office – except for their white unearthly faces, and the indelible blue scars from cuts filled with coal, that look like tattoos across their noses.

A miner near the coal face had said, 'They're only keeping the pits open to keep us in work. If they're giving us charity, do we have to risk our necks for it?' When Orwell went down a pit, he wrote, 'In the metabolism of the Western world the coal-miner is second in importance only to the man who ploughs the soil. He is a sort of grimy caryatid upon whose shoulders everything that is not grimy is supported.' Mining was vital, and heroic. That was some compensation. But now the miners, grinding away their lives in the dark are scarcely more than a burden on the economy. The National Coal Board is in the red. The government subsidizes miners and tries to cushion them against the dangers of an increasing lack of demand for coal. The largest coal consumers are the power stations, all of which if reorganized could be more economically run in the long term on oil or nuclear power. The import of cheaper coal from Poland is banned. Almost all coal by-products can be made more cheaply in other ways.

The dangers of accident and disease alone make it one of the worst jobs in the country. According to the official figures, for 1969 there were 300,000 miners in England. There were 624 new cases of pneumoconiosis. Eighty-two men were killed, over 570 people were seriously injured, and over 111,000 men suffered reportable injuries. Every year mines become safer and better places to work in but mining is a dangerous business. About one in three miners have an accident or industrial disease every year.

A life time on shift work is hard with alternate weeks on mornings, afternoons and nights. Either you start work at five in the morning, or you work till nine at night or you work all night and sleep all day. Like most people who have worked shifts all their lives, the miners say they are used to it and they don't notice it any more. One can get used to most things if there is no alternative.

Coming away from the mine it was hard to believe that underneath the cars, the railway lines, the girls waiting at the bus stop, the supermarket and the traffic lights were men half a mile down crawling on their bellies in galleries two feet high, to scrape out coal that nobody really wants.

Chapter Nine

# Steel

Reg and Mary Atkinson have lived in Rotherham all their lives. They live in one of a row of jerry-built pensioners' bungalows called Jubilee Cottages, up on a hill in Brinsworth within smelling distance of the chemical factory. The house belongs to Steel Peech and Tozer, the biggest steel works in Rotherham, where Reg Atkinson worked from the age of thirteen until he retired at sixty-five, nine years ago.

I stayed with them while I was in Rotherham. Reg's life still revolved around the firm as much as possible. The annual Christmas dinner for old employees is the high spot of his year. 'Steelo's (local name for Steel Peech and Tozer) have done everything for me. They're the best employers. They've been good to me and they're great people to work for,' he will say.

He had to go to work at thirteen to help his family, as he had four brothers and four sisters. He was working on the office side of the firm as a trainee office boy, hoping to better himself. But the family needed more money so he transferred to a higher paid job in the works, with no prospects. He became a paint boy. It was his job to paint the casting numbers on the steel stocks. One day he crawled under a carriage that began to move, and his right hand was completely crushed. All his fingers were amputated. He received only a tiny amount of compensation, partly because he shouldn't have been where he was at the time of the accident. But he was guaranteed a job for life with the firm. 'Not all firms would have done that,' he says, with surprising gratitude. That sort of loyalty to a firm which smashed his hand, gave him one monotonous job to do for the whole of the fifty-two years he was there, and then left him with no more than twenty-six shillings a week pension, is hard to understand.

All Reg's friends had worked in steel, as had most of his relations. Although he was retired his habits still revolved around the shift work timetable. He would still often get up at the crack of dawn and meal times in the household varied. Most of Rotherham is geared to shift work. It is part of the way of life, and has existed in the steel industry and in the mines for generations. In some of the neighbouring pensioners' bungalows, families had stuck to it, more or less, long after retirement. 'First your father is on shifts so the house is run like that, then for fifty years you are on shifts, so it's not a habit to be got out of so easy,' one old steel worker explained. A great deal of their conversation was about steel, the old firm, and the new methods that they had heard about. The drama and importance of steel had entered into their blood. The only significance which they had been able to attach to their own existence, the only place they could claim in a society that by and large makes most of its workers feel expendable, was the fact that they were engaged on work of undeniable national importance.

Steel, as they will tell you, is the root of all things. Houses, offices, ships, new factories, schools, anything that appears in any party's manifesto at election time, depends on the continuing flow of steel. Depends on the men of Rotherham, Scunthorpe or Middlesborough continuing to sweat out the days and nights of their lives in searing heat and appalling danger.

The nobility of work is a bizarre concept. In all the jobs I saw and did, in almost all of the jobs for the working classes, I found little that wasn't stultifying, and degrading to any normal human intelligence. The work itself in the melting shop of a steel works, is not very different from any other, and yet for the first time, I came across people with quite a different attitude towards it. It was partly the sense of responsibility, the feeling that their work was important. Partly it was the excitement, the danger itself. I don't think it would be wrong to suppose that the beauty and the power had something to do with it. I couldn't understand it at all until I went there myself, and saw.

Reg had never been back to the works since he retired. He had wanted to be taken round, to see the modern machinery and to get another look at the old place; at his leaving ceremony he was traditionally invited to return when he liked, but he hadn't really thought they meant it. He was excited, and, I think, as astounded as I was. One would never guess he'd worked there most of his life.

The melting shop at Steelo's was the most beautiful, the most terrifying, the most breath-taking sight I have ever seen. High up on the metal catwalk we gazed down in silence for a long time. It was the biggest building I had ever been in, dark with no windows, and dim lights far up above in the ceiling. Every piece of machinery was so vast that the tiny furnacemen milling about below didn't seem to be controlling it at all, a place for fiery giants but not for human beings. The size and noise filled one with fear.

Up there on the catwalk was like a nightmare – like balancing on a tight rope above the jaws of hell. The bright orange glares, the fire spitting and shooting out goblets of white molten steel and sending them scudding across the floor, the rivulets of blue, grey and vermilion slag pouring out of the furnaces, the unearthly colours and the unceasing roar of the fires. We stood and watched.

There were six furnaces like huge black tea cups and each one the size of a two storey house. Giant metal ladles as big as a room, carried the scrap steel along a rail and filled up the furnaces. The lid was slid across and into each furnace, three electrodes, great columns the thickness of a pillar of the Parthenon, were slowly lowered. When the electrodes hit the scrap metal, the noise was unbelievable. The metal expands and crackles, and the whole great shop is rent with a sound like a thousand bombs exploding at once. The electrodes turn white and blue with the heat, and through the holes at the bottom of the furnaces, the fires spit out their flames. Soon more doors in the furnaces are opened and all the impurities from the paint on old bicycle frames, the rust on old railings, simmer to the top and ooze out into troughs in the concrete floor.

'Even now,' said our guide, 'whenever I come into the melting shop I am amazed. It's a very splendid thing.' He was a man in his late thirties who had worked all his life as a bricklayer in the melting shop. The furnaces are lined with fire bricks, which have to be replaced all the time. He had recently been promoted to a staff job in the personnel department. 'Every man on the floor down there will tell you with pride that this is the biggest electric arc melting shop in the world,' he said.

After the metal has been melted and when it is almost ready to be 'tapped', (tipped out and poured into moulds), oxygen is plunged into the middle of the molten mass to bring the temperature up even higher at the last moment. It is thrust in through one of the doors at the bottom of the furnace, and this is one of the most dangerous operations of all. The oxygen is liable to back fire, and to shoot out of the door into the shop. This happened while we were watching. A sheet of flame roared out of the furnace to a distance of twenty yards or so. That flame is of an unimaginable heat. Anyone hit by it probably wouldn't even have time to know what had happened to him. There are men working at the doors, right up close to the furnaces, taking samples and watching what is going on. They are also likely to be hit at any time by the thousands of little lumps like sparks that are spat out and sometimes carry quite a long distance. The furnaces are in one long line, and the furnacemen walk around in front of them, apparently quite unconcerned. Later one of them explained, 'There wouldn't be time to run. I just try not to worry, and most of the time I forget about the danger.'

I was then taken down on to the floor, a rare privilege for visitors. We climbed down the metal staircase, flight by flight, all the way to the bottom. Looking up at them, the furnaces looked even bigger and even more threatening. You can't help being aware that almost all the time you are within direct firing range of one or other of the furnaces, should any of them choose that moment to belch out a sheet of flame, or a lethal scattering of sparks. It was hot, but not as hot as I had expected. The furnacemen were wearing thick dark blue flannel shirts, cool, I was told, as they absorb the sweat. Sudden bursts of heat hit you as you walk past the open furnace doors. I got no nearer than five yards or so, but there were men standing within inches of them, plunging irons into the molten metal to collect samples for the laboratory. They shielded their faces with their arms, and turned their heads away. It was like pulling a tooth from the jaws of a dragon. They had glass visors on their helmets, but I never saw any of them use one. Even where I was standing, with my face turned away as far as I could, the heat was searing on the skin, and painful. Most furnacemen have burnt faces, as well as a number of small scars, little pits in the flesh from tiny sparks. All the men on the floor have large ear-muffs fitted to their helmets too, but again, no one used them when I was there. They keep them stuck on the top of their helmets like a spare pair of ears. 'The trouble is,' said a shop steward I spoke to on the floor, 'we get used to the noise quite quickly, and there doesn't seem any point in wearing those things. You can't hear people talk, and they're hot on the ears. A lot of people suffer quite serious ear damage from working here. Everyone knows that, but they still don't bother.' There are tests for noise level every six months.

The whole place is covered with a thick red dust, iron oxide. Although there are extractors, a great deal of it still belches out into the air from the huge chimneys above the furnaces and the air in the melting shop is full of it.

Some of the processes in the shop are televised on closed circuit, and a lot of the running of it is computerized. The computer is fed data collected from the specimens of metal drawn from the furnaces during melting, and it issues instructions. Besides each furnace is a cabin where the furnacemen sit when they have a few minutes off, and where all the controls are, including elaborate intercom devices so that the crane drivers and cradle operators can be given instructions as efficiently as possible. In fact I noticed that most of the operations that require any delicate handling are all done in the old way, by gesture. A furnaceman stands where he can see the furnace and the crane driver and he waves his arms at the driver, beckoning, calling a halt, or edging him to one side as he carefully lowers the electrodes into the slot on top of the furnace.

There are a number of notices everywhere reading, 'Do not loiter' and 'Walk fast'. I wanted to run, and keep running, but everyone else was calm. People were ambling around, even stopping to chat in places I was afraid to scuttle past.

In one of the cabins, surrounded by control panels and dials, a few furnacemen were sitting huddled together drinking tea. By tradition furnacemen have always drunk huge amounts of beer to counteract the heat and the sweating. This has changed now. The companies used to provide each man with a daily ration. 'You couldn't drink as much water as you need,' one of them explained, 'but you can get down a lot of beer more easily.' They tipped their helmets back from their burnt faces. A shop steward was sitting there at the time, a large man, strong and gentle. 'Aren't you frightened?' I asked him. 'Yes, of course,' he said smiling. 'We're all frightened most of the time. You get used to it. I mean you get used to being frightened, you don't get used to the danger.' He paused for a moment and added, 'It's probably a good thing. It stops a man being careless.'

The manager who was showing me round said that the average wage on the melting shop floor was £35 a week. Some men would earn considerably more. 'It's above the national average for the steel industry here,' the shop steward said. I asked him about shift work. How did they feel about the irregularity of their lives, the strange hours and upside down days. 'We've never known different,' he answered, surprised by my question. 'As children we'll all tell you about tiptoeing round the house with no shoes on because Dad's asleep, being turned out of the house if we whispered, watching him eat his meals at all hours, and sometimes he'd have whole afternoons with time to play with us. It's just a fact of life, like it or not.' We looked out of the window of the cabin where one of the great furnaces was being tapped. Slowly it was tipped up to an angle of 45 degrees and the molten steel streamed out, the whole shop aglow, the chimneys roaring. No one spoke. They seemed almost as startled and awe-struck by the sight as I was. Eventually he turned and said, 'We all know it has to go on. Steel has to be made. These new electric furnaces can't stop for a moment in the working week. How could we all go home for a good night's sleep and switch them off?' The machines ran their lives and they seemed quite to accept that their lives should be spent in feeding and tending these splendid great giants. It didn't seem to be the employers so much as the furnaces that made such tremendous demands on them. They live like a tribe at the foot of a volcano, placating a hungry fiery god with elaborate and dangerous rituals.

They were proud of the furnaces, of the whole melting shop. 'The fact that steel is vital, that what we do here matters, that it's really needed by everyone everywhere, I think that's in most furnaceman's minds too,' said one man. Here were men working in fear, in almost continual danger, and heat, forced to sleep in the day and work at night one week in three, threatened by redundancy with each of the great technical advances, that they were praising, talking about pride in their work, and a sense of purpose. I hadn't in any of the other places I had been to heard anyone say anything like it before. The drama of making steel in the biggest electric arc melting shop in the world seemed to sweep over most obstacles to their happiness. They sounded like new recruits on their way to the front. Or more surprising still, men at the front who were still talking like the new recruits who hadn't got there yet.

'In the old days,' said the shop steward, 'you'd have found some miners saying the same things about their work, when mining was an essential industry. Now for them it's nothing but a dreadful job.' He paused for a moment and stubbed out his cigarette quite viciously into an old tin lid. 'It'll be the same with us very soon. They make steel cheaper in other countries. I suppose the government will protect us from that for a while. But when you're protected, you begin to know it's charity. And then soon no one's going to want steel. They say they can make plastics now that are stronger than steel, and cheaper. What's going to happen to us? We look at the mines and we feel in our bones that it won't be long.'

In spite of the loyalty and enthusiasm of some of the steel workers, the old ones and the better paid furnacemen in particular, there is no getting away from the fact that their life is to most people, a peculiar sort of unadulterated hell. Because they are used to it, and because they've been more or less born into it, it is easy for people to say, 'But they're happy. They wouldn't want to do anything else.' That doesn't seem to me to be any answer at all. If I went up to a sweaty exhausted steel worker, standing within inches of an unpredictable furnace that might at any moment annihilate him with one fiery blast and said, 'Don't you wish you were the editor of the *New Statesman*? Wouldn't you like to have had a fellowship to All Soul's?' What would he say? He would stare at me with utter incomprehension. His horizons have been stretched no further than what is reasonably within his grasp. Phrased another way, I might ask 'What other kind of work would you like to have done? Is there any job or any way of life you would rather have had?' The answer would probably have gone like this: 'Well, I never was very good at school. I couldn't get out of there quick enough. I lived in Rotherham, and at fifteen lived with my parents, so I looked around here for a job. My father was in steel. The money's good if you work hard, and in those days there were very good prospects for the future of the industry. I wouldn't want to go down the pit, and anyway that's a dying business.' And that would seem a very reasonable assessment of his chances. To say that he liked and was happy in his work is to say that he is not positively unhappy. Very few people are. The human mind is resilient and accepting. I do not think it patronizing or interfering to look at people who are in jobs that they cannot be said in any real way to have chosen, and to say that they are not happy.

If all the people who have had little control over their destiny and are now in dead-end jobs, living in horrible towns all over the country, suddenly became aware that their intelligence had been more or less determined at the age of three by their poor environment, that their education had been geared to streaming them into appropriate categories to fill the needs of industry and society, that however comprehensive their children's education might be, they stand no real chance of having a very different life either, that their standard of living will rise at an increasingly low rate, and that the gap between themselves and the rich is likely to widen and not to narrow, there would be revolution. It is not just because people do not realize these facts and the full significance of them, that they do not rebel. It is because the facts are too unbearable to face up to. Who would really believe that they have no power over their own destiny? Predestination has always been the hardest doctrine to swallow, and anyone telling them that they never had a choice is likely to get punched in the jaw.

We all live happily because we are prepared to believe a network of lies, and conflicting half truths. We couldn't bear to be without them. Hypocrisy is a necessary part of life and politics and not to be condemned especially. The resistance to the Freudian doctrine comes from much the same resentment towards any total view of the world that claims that our lives have been predetermined by a force, or a parent utterly outside our control.

On the other hand, to say 'If the workers are happy, what does it matter? If the wool is pulled over their eyes and they don't mind, who are we to complain on their behalf?' is another thing altogether. The workers are not miserable, but they are not happy. Most of the workers I spoke to were saying that they were bored with their work, that they would have liked to be different, that they hoped things would have changed for their children, or maybe for their grandchildren. They knew more or less that they had had a bad deal from society and that all the 'good' and 'worthwhile' things they had heard about in school were not really for the likes of them. Of course this is greatly over simplified, but there is no doubt that there are and there will be for a very long time, a large number of jobs that require little skill and almost no intelligence that have to be filled. There are also a large number of children at school coming into contact for the only time in their lives with 'middle class' ideas of the satisfactions that can be got out of life on whom these ideas are not even supposed to have any effect, over and beyond making them reasonably good citizens. While the jobs are there, the people have got to be produced to do them. You can't educate away the problem.

Chapter Ten

# Old Age

And at the end of it all, when you've done your stint and paid your taxes, paid your union dues and your insurance stamp, when you've buried your parents and married your children, what have you got to look forward to in the next ten or more years?

It was a Wednesday afternoon in January and on Wednesdays Reg and Mary Atkinson went down the road to the Darby and Joan club. There was bustling around Jubilee Cottages. Ice was thick on the ground, and the old people had to walk down a steep hill to get to the parish hall. Some said they couldn't manage it, afraid of slipping, or of the smog that was thicker than usual over Brinsworth. Reg suggested that I should come to the club too. 'We've never really enough people,' he said, 'and they're always glad to see young faces.' So I agreed to go.

Wrapping up in thick clothes and rubber shoes, everyone set off. In the end only the Mitchells next door didn't go. He had lost half one leg in the steel works and didn't trust himself on the ice.

The temperature inside the hall was barely different to the temperature outside. There was no question of anyone's taking off their coats. They stamped their feet and made jokes and huddled up to each other at the tables that had been set round the room.

The hall was quite big, and prefabricated. More like a Nissen hut than anything, built in the war and hollow underfoot. You could feel the floor boards bending and the echoes and noises from people walking around added to the bleak chilliness of the place. There were two electric fires set high on the wall but they did hardly more than keep the ice off the insides of the windows.

The old people were looking round the room to see who was there. They were not in fact very old, or at least, if they were, they were all very spry. 'Not many come today. Must be the weather,' said an old lady sitting next to me. 'There's usually more of us, or a few more anyhow.' There must have been about thirty people there, and noticeably more women than men. 'We always look around a little nervous at first,' said Mary. 'You never know who's gone in the week.'

From a room at the side came a large woman in her fifties wearing a flowered overall, red faced and beaming. 'Afternoon boys and girls, ladies and gentlemen!' she said. 'Are we all here?' There was some shuffling around and they all answered. 'No, Flo's not come,' and 'Edna and Albert aren't here.' She rubbed her hands together in the cold and said, 'Shall we wait a bit longer for them?' They all said 'Yes.' But no one else came, and the room did seem empty.

'Right now boys and girls, let's have our song shall we?' said the lady in the floral overall. After coughs and clearings of rusty throats and wheezings, like the starting up of an organ, their timid voices, mixed with a few cracked baritones, sang out this song.

Just like Darby and Joan
In a world of our own
We'll build a nest
Out in the West.
Be it so humble
We'll never grumble.
After Summer has flown
And the grey locks have shown
Age may betide us
But love will guide us
Just like Darby and Joan.

A sadder, more resigned and defeated song is hard to imagine. These old people hadn't much in life when they were young, and now they had nothing, except resignation and acceptance of their lot.

They stood for the Lord's prayer and sat down to a few rounds of gin rummy, with chewed-up old cards.

The lady in the overall clapped her hands twice and called out, 'Right now boys and girls, put the cards away when you've finished your game. It's time for bingo.' There was some excitement and people packed away their cards. Bingo was the high spot of the club. A man called Henry stepped neatly forward to call out the bingo numbers. It was a much sought after job. 'Reg used to do it till a few months ago,' Henry's wife whispered to me. 'But he can't manage it so good since he had that heart attack. He was playing dominoes down here at the time. He just slumped over the table and we all thought he'd gone.'

'Come on Henry, me old flower,' said the lady. 'Let's have the numbers.' He sat down at the table at one end of the room. 'Give us some luck, Henry.' 'Be nice to me this time, Henry,' they all joked, until he called out, 'Eyes Down!'

The prize was fifteen pence. They were poor enough for this to add some pleasant luxury to the winner's week, an extra ten cigarettes, a cake for tea. 'Kelly's eye, number one. On its own number three. Unlucky for some, number thirteen. Legs eleven.' There were wolf whistles all round the room, part of the bingo tradition. 'Blind twenty,' and so on. Bingo is a fairly new addition to these old people's lives but a foreigner might have thought it was the oldest English ritual of all to see them play.

'Come on Henry old friend. Give me a break!' 'You're rotten Henry, you never call mine,' the banter went on, amidst laughs and nudgings. Then someone shouted 'Bingo!' and there were claps and groans. The cards and counters were collected up and it was time for tea.

Check table cloths were laid over the ink stained trestles and the two women who always did teas went off to the kitchen. 'Mind you,' Ivy was saying to me, 'Sheffield's better than Rotherham for the old. We used to get free transport from six in the morning to three in the afternoon but now they let you go free until nine at night. That's so you can visit your friends in hospital of an evening. But you can't go outside a small area – in Sheffield it's all free and you go where you like.' The tea was brought in, a big battered urn, and plates of plain sponge.

'One thing we don't do much of here,' Ivy said, with a wheezy laugh, 'We don't like to ask each other how we are. You get such a dreadful list of complaints.'

Tea over, there was a raffle. The prizes were a bag of sugar and a packet of tea. There was dominoes and cards and then another round of bingo. The prize this time was six eggs. Another quick prayer and it was time to go home. 'I know it's not much, but it's quite something to look forward to in the week,' Mary Atkinson said as we buttoned our coats. 'You don't get to see people much, and it's nice to be out of the house.'

We walked slowly back up the hill. It was colder and more slippery under foot. The bungalow was icy cold when we got in. The only heating in the house was the small gas fire in the sitting room which was turned off to save money whenever they went out. The house consisted of a tiny kitchen, a sitting room, a bathroom and a bedroom. It should, I suppose, have been ideal. It was specially built by the company for its retired employees. But with a scrubby bit of waste land in front and behind, situated on a slope that any amateur eye could see would be bad for drainage, it was bleak and grim. In the middle of the industrial area, near the chemical works and well within belching distance of other factory chimneys, far from the shops, no one would have chosen the spot for old people. It was so damp that water would sometimes seep through the floor boards and flood the kitchen. There was hot water, but the immersion heater had no thermostat, so it had to be turned off all the time. 'We couldn't afford it anyway,' Mary said. 'We only turn it on for baths. The rest of the time we heat water in kettles.' They were quite a new row of cottages, and the steel company was probably proud of them, probably showed their foreign business visitors round. They looked good outside, but if they'd been built for the council, I don't think the contractor would ever have got another job. They were shoddy, cold, and so thin-walled that you could hear the people next door turn over in bed.

Reg and Mary get a combined pension from the state of £9.70 a week. He receives £1.30 a week from 'Steelo's'. They pay £2 a week for gas and electricity and 30p rent (which is very considerably less than most pensioners have to pay in ordinary flats). Then there is the television rental of 50p a week, plus 15p towards the licence. Then there is a small death pension (to bury them when they die). This leaves a total of £7.95 for food, clothes, travel, clubs, and 'all the things that go wrong in the house all the time'. For two people to live on, that is very little money indeed. And it is as much as two or three pounds more than a great many old age pensioners have.

Mary Atkinson's household budget for the week is easy to calculate. She knows exactly what she spends, almost down to the last penny. Otherwise they wouldn't manage. Out of the £7.95 left after rent, heat, gas and television she spends:

| | |
|---|---|
| Meat (mostly bacon, sausages, chops) | £1.60 |
| Cheese | 16 |
| Milk | 38 |
| Potatoes | 12½ |
| 1 dozen eggs | 21 |
| Greens | 25 |
| ½lb Butter/½lb marg | 27½ |
| Tea/coffee | 18 |
| Bread | 42 |
| Breakfast cereal | 12 |
| Flour | 14 |
| Groceries (sugar, salt, pepper, mustard, jam, cocoa etc) | 26 |
| Soap powder | 6 |
| Soap | 5 |
| Medical supplies (aspirin, corn plasters, etc.) | 32 |
| Cigarettes (10 a day for Reg) | 91 |
| Whistdrive/clubs, bingo | 50 |
| Saved for holidays | 40 |
| One pint of beer on Sunday for Reg | 14 |
| Football pools | 15 |
| Miscellaneous (travel, clothes, household utensils, breakages, polish, hairdresser etc.) | 1.30 |
| | £7.95 |

It marks quite a severe drop in their standard of living. When he was earning, their life would not have been too hard. With only one hand, he was not a highly paid worker, and they had three children, but they didn't have to scrimp and ponder over every penny they had. They never had enough money to put much by, or to get a mortgage. No one could point a finger at them and accuse them of fecklessness. Those who did manage, through some hardship, to save something while they were working, have found themselves in more or less the same situation and they have had to swallow the bitter pill of seeing the hard saved pounds become worth nothing like the sacrifice they made at the time. A life on £7 a week, this is what all working people can look forward to when they retire.

In every way Reg and Mary's lives were circumscribed by privation, nearly all of which was due to lack of money. Their old friends lived far away, and so did most of their relations. By being partitioned off in an old people's colony, they were forced to make the best of their neighbours, whether they liked them or not. 'Everyone is always wondering who'll be the next to go. They're a terrible morbid lot. Mr Mitchell next door, grumbles and moans all day long. I know he has half a leg missing, but Reg never fusses, with his hand. There's nothing really wrong with him, he just likes to be ill. When people move in here they all feel they're going to die soon, or something. And his wife, Enid. We play cards with her often in the evening for pennies. But she cheats. She revokes at whist all the time. Well, we can't say anything about it. We're stuck with them.'

By a curious coincidence, as she was talking there was a scuffling outside the kitchen door, and then a quick knock. Mrs Blackwell was standing there sniffing with a handkerchief in her hand, but she wasn't really crying. 'Mabel's gone,' she said. 'I thought I'd come and tell you right now, Mary.' Mary asked her in and made cups of tea.

Mrs Blackwell told her story. Mabel was a widow who lived down the road. It was a bad winter for 'flu and she caught it. The doctor came to see her and told her to stay in bed. People dropped in on her from time to time to bring her soup and food, and she got better, so they stopped calling. Then the milkman saw she hadn't taken in her milk for a couple of days and he looked through the letter box. He saw her sprawled half in and half out of an arm chair and called the police. She'd been there for nearly three days.

'Mrs Blackwell loves gossip,' Mary said when she'd gone. 'She's rushing all down the road telling everyone. She's one of those that loves bad news. The worse the news the happier she is.'

An old people's ghetto is a dismal world, particularly for strong and lively people like the Atkinsons. But you're lucky if you manage to die on your feet in a place like that, rather than rot to death in an old people's home or worse still, a geriatric ward. With a little planning, with a little care, couldn't old people's flats easily be built into the community? It is always being discussed but hardly ever happens. They wouldn't have to be pushed out on their own. Quite apart from the inhumanity of treating them like that, it is a terrible future for any worker to have ahead of him. True, most workers probably don't think about it any more than people think about death, but when it comes to the point, when you're working hard at a soul-destroying job and you long to get out of it, retirement might be something to look forward to, not to dread. With a good deal more money, and more consideration, retirement could be the bonus at the end of the day. It should be the time when there are no worries about money and children, no work to be done. And as the retirement age is getting lower, and life expectation higher, it could be a time for beginning new life and new occupations.

Reg lives in the past. He talks about work and the firm. At night he stands by the window and looks down towards the steel works. As a great yellow glare strikes up into the sky, same time every night, he plunges his fists deeper into his pockets and says, in the same voice of longing, 'They're tapping down int' Steelos.'

On the mantel-piece is a big ornate modern clock with a glass base and gold coloured trimmings. Inside the base there are four gold balls, and for hour after hour, day after day, the balls swing round in a three quarter circle, pause for a fraction of a second, and swing back. Forward, pause, back, forward, pause, back, in an unending mesmerising rhythm. Its effect on the room, placed firmly in the centre, is to concentrate everyone's attention on it. Only the television distracts the eye from the clock. The Steel Company gives one of these clocks to all its employees when they retire. It only needs winding every 400 days.

'I don't like winding it,' Reg said with half a laugh. 'I always wonder if I'll ever wind it up again.'

Once a week he takes down the big stainless steel plaque on

the wall, 'For services to Steel Peech and Tozer from 1907 to 1957'. 'If my fifty years had come two years later, I'd have got a stainless steel tea service, with a stainless steel tray,' Reg said, resting it on his bad arm and polishing it with a duster with his good hand. 'But I think I like the plaque better.'

# Note

For some of the jobs that I did I needed the co-operation of the management as they were not the sort of places that employed casual labour. Lever Brothers and Joseph Lucas Ltd both gave me their full co-operation. To the best of my knowledge, while I was working there only the top management and personnel officers in these two factories knew what I was doing there. Neither the workers nor the foremen were told.

The National Coal Board and the Steel Corporation both arranged for me to be taken round and to meet workers. The Department of Employment arranged for me to be present at the interviews at Labour Exchanges, the school and the Youth Employment Bureaux.

Bird's Eye in Grimsby, Fords at Dagenham and the G.P.O. telephone service all refused to let me work and write about them.

# About the Author

Polly Toynbee was born on the Isle of Wight and brought up in London. She was educated at Holland Park Comprehensive School and St Anne's College, Oxford. She is now a journalist with *The Guardian* and *The Sunday Times*, and is married to Peter Jenkins, the political columnist and Washington correspondent of *The Guardian*. They have two daughters.

Polly Toynbee is the daughter of Philip Toynbee, the critic and journalist, and the granddaughter of Arnold Toynbee, the famous historian.

## Some Penguins you might enjoy

FOR WHOM THE BELL TOLLS Ernest Hemingway
A KESTREL FOR A KNAVE Barry Hines
WHISKY GALORE Compton Mackenzie
BUDDENBROOKS Thomas Mann
CIDER WITH ROSIE Laurie Lee
AS I WALKED OUT ONE MIDSUMMER MORNING Laurie Lee
OF HUMAN BONDAGE W. Somerset Maugham
NO ROOM IN THE ARK Alan Moorehead
1066 AND ALL THAT W. C. Sellar and R. J. Yeatman
ANIMAL FARM George Orwell
CRY THE BELOVED COUNTRY Alan Paton
BONJOUR TRISTESSE Françoise Sagan
THE PRIME OF MISS JEAN BRODIE Muriel Spark
THE DAUGHTER OF TIME Josephine Tey
THE GRAPES OF WRATH John Steinbeck
BILLY LIAR Keith Waterhouse
THE PICTURE OF DORIAN GRAY Oscar Wilde
THE MIDWICH CUCKOOS John Wyndham
THE BOY FRIEND Sandy Wilson
There is also a Penguin Handbook
CAREERS FOR GIRLS by Ruth Miller